Th3 Simple Questions

Slice Open Everyday Life

JEAN W. YEAGER

Jan-June 2014
Blog Posts From The
threesimplequestions bLog

WESTBOW°
PRESS
A DIVISION OF THOMAS NELSON
& ZONDERVAN

WestBow Press books may be ordered through booksellers or by contacting:

WestBow Press
A Division of Thomas Nelson & Zondervan
1663 Liberty Drive
Bloomington, IN 47403
www.westbowpress.com
1 (866) 928-1240

ISBN: 978-1-4908-7124-0 (sc)
ISBN: 978-1-4908-7125-7 (hc)
ISBN: 978-1-4908-7123-3 (e)

Library of Congress Control Number: 2015903122

Print information available on the last page.

WestBow Press rev. date: 03/19/2015

CONTENTS

ABOUT "TH3 SIMPLE QUESTIONS"

The Simple Questions slice open the stuff of everyday life in which we live and reveals the unseen, mystical, allegorical, emotional, as well as the hidden technologies, and actions corporations hide. This book is a compilation Jan-June 2014 *threesimplequestions* blog posts which drew 10,000 visits from public "social networking" sources.

The way in which the segments were written was very simple: every week, or more frequently, take five minutes and answer these three simple questions: "Who am I?", Why am I here?", and "What do I want?" These three simple questions penetrate like thin knife blades inserted into the heart of everyday life. What bleeds out has been struggles, pain, love, joy, concerns, confusion and some truths.

The writing is an immediate act of composition - free from all rules and artful manipulation. It is intimate and personal, honest and dynamic using creativity to affirm the Human Spirit.

THREE STRANGE ANGELS?
Some have asked about the angelic shapes on the cover. I must admit my muses are three strange angels who have inspired many of these entries. Who are these angels? I am not sure. I first met them in D.H. Lawrence's poem, *"The Song Of The Man Who Has Come Through"*
   I am grateful for their help.

—Jean Yeager, 2014

I AM WHO I AM NOT BUT MAY HAVE BEEN

WHO AM I NOT?

I am who I am not: I am the one who does not speak French or German or Arabic or a host of other languages. I am not afraid to try to learn, but I wouldn't place a large wager on my becoming fluent. I can't even spell very well in English. Opera does not float my boat and neither do boats, though I have owned several small fishing boats over the years. I have no burning desire to go to China or Japan or to the Orient. I won't get up early to stand in line to buy an iPhone, iPad or iGizmo. I am not militaristic. I am not a fan of big corporations or big government. I don't ask people what they think I should do. I don't speak your mind. I try not to meddle in my kids' lives, but I'll leave them free to tell you different. I am not gifted in music, though my mother, bless her soul, kept up the piano lessons until 4th grade. I have a misperception of my capacities to play football and baseball, though I am not afraid to play third base. I am not afraid to make a mistake on my own taxes. I am not afraid to volunteer in maximum security prisons. I am not shy, I am curious. I do not give my time away easily. I do get second opinions when it comes to what doctors tell me.

And so I can make a list of the things I am not: not gifted in, have no desire to do, or have no interest in whatsoever.

WHY AM I HERE?

Much of our culture defines people by their gifts and talents, what you're good at. But what about the things we're not good at, or the list you or I could make based on the above? Why are we NOT interested in those specific things?

I can, and have, made such a list. I take it out and refer to it whenever my wife and I get out our bucket list, or annually, just to see if I've uncovered something else I'm not good at.

If you were someone who thought your soul was a spiritual component that may have lived through multiple lives, you could wonder whether or not from lifetime to lifetime your soul picked up certain capacities, became good at one thing or another. Then, once the soul became good at a thing, like a language or playing music, or third base or what have you, it got it, then the next time around the soul wasn't particularly interested.

Rudolf Steiner (1861-1925), a spiritual scientist, in one of his lectures on reincarnation, suggested that if you entertain that line of operating hypothesis, and conduct your own research, then making a list of what you do not care about, are not good at, and avoid (who you are not in this life) might give you a pointer as to who you may have been in a previous life or in all previous lives. For example, based on my personal research, I could have been a concubine who was also a professional cellist in China, or a brick maker in Egypt or a dancing nose-flute player in Africa.

WHAT DO I WANT?

Can life, or business, be lived according to the Quaker Community Softball Team approach? Or should we continue to push the gifts and talents of people to excel as we now do?

The community team method is to be inclusive and give everyone the opportunity to play. It asks overly technical and talented people to develop a feeling for emotions and love. It asks lovers to smarten up a bit, musicians to put down the cello and pick up the t-square.

It asks the ones who are, as Paul Simon said, "soft in the middle" to get a little firmer and those who are too firm in the middle to soften. It gives everybody a chance to play. It is not outcome based.

This kind of thinking leads to weird mental constructs and experiences. I could add here a great personal story about my Quaker softball team which went 100% defeated for an entire season. Our record came down to the last at bat of the last game. Impossibly we were tied and had the bases loaded in the bottom of the last inning with our autistic catcher up to bat. She got w-a-y too happily excited. I have never, and probably will NEVER, see a human being so excited and so excarnated as that young woman was. It was worth the price of admission to life to watch that. My, my, my. And we managed to muff the opportunity to score a run, so in the end, we kept our perfect season: 0 and 10.

I can hear the voices of my overly hard friends speaking in my mental ears, chastising me once again for that wishy-washy kind of view of life, and business, they know I enjoy.

But that raises another question. Why in the world do I pick the friends I do!? WE do. They seem to be the ones who are constantly trying to better me/us, push me/us, correct me/us, keep me/us from slipping into my/our comfortable easy chairs of life and disappearing into my/ourselves. They are very much at work helping me/us become more like the person I/we am/are not. Thank you.

(Note to self: Do not apply the Quaker Softball Community Team approach to pronouns ever again!)

SOME OF US ESCAPED

WHO WERE WE?

We were raised on fairytales, loose parts and pocket knives. Our breakfast cereal was robbery served in cardboard refrigerator boxes. We treasured potential-filled junk. We were inventors, heroes, bad guys, prisoners and monsters. Someone suffered, tragically. There were bruises earned by freedom and exploration. We lunched on possibilities and inspiration. We roamed mountain tops and captured flags. We hated, conspired, plotted, and betrayed. We explored the bitterness of guilt and discovered the sweet capacity to forgive. We suffered courageously, dangerously and creatively.

WHY WERE WE HERE?

Life began to sort us out in childhood. We moved into self-selected groups like animals herding. The loud ones over THERE! Frightened? Here. Ruthless? There. Kind? Stay with me. We found one another. Then we were sent to the teachers. They took away our mountain tops and gave us playground slides, one-way journeys. They wanted us to behave. Stick to task. Then our parents, who were modern, thought life needed goals. So childhood became about accomplishment. They led some kids away to nurture their gifts and pushed them into molds of rules, white lines and competition. You're not good at this. Try that. Specialization. Careers. They tried to get us all. Even pirates or pretend bad guys got labeled and sorted.

WHAT DO WE WANT?

Some of us escaped, somehow. We didn't fit into the mold. We became the risk takers, start-up founders, the entrepreneurs and craftspeople. Lots of musicians and artists. The creatives. We have dinner with the others, who live in their carefully crafted skill-sets, follow their career paths and retirement plans. We envy their stability; they envy our uniqueness. They talk excitedly about bonus-mile trips to the mountains. We suggest we have a mountain right here and that we should get together and tackle heroin use in the neighborhood. They say rules, white lines, and uniforms. We say suffer courageously, dangerously and creatively. My friend says "upgrades." I whisper "pocket knives."

WILLIAM SHAKESPEARE AND YOU DREAM EACH OTHER

WHO AM I?

Writers are dreamers who gather imagination and fantasies and bring them down to words. When the reader reads what I have written, you read and imagine or experience my dream, and so you dream along with me. You follow along with my thinking and my path through the fantasies to the imagination.

So, as a writer, I must be aware that the reader and I share an intimate, sacred space. I must be true to the reader. Because you follow my imagination, my interior becomes your interior; my passions, your passions (even if only for a while). I must be very careful about what I write because it is not only for my self-expression but because what I write goes into your soul.

It all begins with the writer's dream and the reader's willingness to dream along with him.

When William Shakespeare wrote sonnets to his lover, he was a writer gathering imagination and fantasies and bringing them down to words on paper. But the words expressed an intimacy and knowledge of the lover not known to the ordinary reader. And when his lover read his writing, she dreamt his dream in a more intimate way. She followed along with his thinking and his path through his intimate fantasies to the imagination.

As a writer, he was aware that the reader/lover and he shared an intensely intimate, sacred space. He was very careful about what he wrote because the response was more highly charged and evocative for his lover than it is for us readers hundreds of years later.

WHY AM I HERE?

The reader or dreamer of the writer's dream has what may be called a Night Self consciousness versus a Day Self consciousness. The Day Self consciousness begins when you wake in the morning and drag your emotions and body out of bed and ends when you go to sleep at night. The Day Self consciousness is sense-bound. When the Day Self lies down to rest the body and the energetic self, your Night Self arises and unfolds. This is a deeper sleeping than the reader's sleep.

The Day Self believes that all of life is measured by its accomplishments, the stuff of your to-do list, what you post on Facebook and tuck into photo albums (the resumes, degrees, awards, milestones along the concentric circles of your life, including business trips, family carpooling, small-town worries, shopping and Starbucks, culminating in a headstone).

The Day Self exists in space; the Night Self exists in time. Her existence is measured in cycles of time, rhythmical patterns, seasonal revels, festivals, evolution, joy, warm welcomes, canning, gardens, growth, children and all expressions of love. The night reveals a world qualitatively different from the experience of the day.

Shakespeare's Sonnet XLIII is the dream in which the dreamer meets the lover in the night. This is a dreamer writing the dream in which he describes the Dream Lover.

> "When most I wink, then do mine eyes best see,
> For all the day they view things unrespected;
> But when I sleep, in dreams they look on thee,
> And darkly bright are bright in dark directed.
> Then thou, whose shadow shadows doth make bright,
> How would thy shadow's form form happy show
> To the clear day with thy much clearer light,

When to unseeing eyes thy shade shines so?
How would, I say, my eyes be blessed made
By looking on thee in the living day,
When in dead night thy fair imperfect shade
Through heavy sleep on sightless eyes doth stay!
All days are nights to see till I see thee,
And nights bright days when dreams do show thee me."

When, hundreds of years after it was written, you read Shakespeare's dream of the Dream Lover, a mood of the night remains. A feeling, perhaps. Not the stuff of Day consciousness.

WHAT DO I WANT?

We are all sleepers in the dreams of others. Before you were born, lofty spiritual beings dreamed you into existence. Where are they now? Who is dreaming the dream of you? Who is writing your story? Whose ideals or ideas fill your inner world? Where do you go when you sleep? With whom do you commune? Who is it that dreams that "deep and dreamless sleep" as silent stars go by over the little town of Bethlehem? When, where and why will we awaken, lose our illusions or become disenchanted?

WHAT WILL BECOME OF THEM? *GHOST OF CHRISTMAS PRESENT AND EBENEZER SCROOGE*

Excerpts from *A Christmas Carol*, by Charles Dickens (1812-1870), interwoven with recent news digests, June 2014.

Unaccompanied Children (UACs) are an unprecedented surge of young immigrants at the southern Texas and Arizona border.

"'I am the Ghost of Christmas Present,' said the Spirit. 'Look upon me.'

"Scrooge did so. It was clothed in one simple green robe or mantle, bordered with white fur. This garment hung so loosely on the figure, that its capacious breast was bare, as if disdaining to be warded or concealed by any artifice. Its feet, observable beneath the ample folds of the garment were also bare; and on its head it wore no other covering than a holly wreath, set here and there with shining icicles. Its dark brown curls were long and free; free as its genial face, its sparkling eye, its open hand, its cheery voice, its unconstrained demeanor, and its joyful air. Girded round its middle was an antique sword scabbard; but no sword was in it, and the ancient sheath was eaten up with rust."

Overcrowding, at the Texas border, has meant that the UACs are being transported to other facilities, such as military bases. FEMA is coordinating the large scale effort, with HHS handling housing and care through the Office of Refugee Resettlement.

"...it was a long night, if it were only a night; but Scrooge had his doubts of this, because the Christmas holidays appeared to be condensed into the space of time they passed together. It was strange, too, that while Scrooge remained unaltered in his outward form, the Ghost grew older, clearly older...."

Others have fled their countries because they feared danger in their home countries due to narco-terrorist gangs, traffickers and criminals.

"'Are spirits' lives so short?' asked Scrooge."

They risked the flight north and the dangers of crossing the open desert at night only to face arrest and detention upon illegal entry into the U.S.

"'My life upon this globe is very brief,' replied the Ghost. 'It ends tonight.'"

WHAT IS THE GIFT OF THE GHOST OF CHRISTMAS PRESENT?

"'Forgive me if I am not justified in what I ask,' said Scrooge, looking intently at the Spirit's robe, 'but I see something strange, and not belonging to yourself, protruding from under your skirts. Is it a foot or claw?'"

Some blogs and news stories have estimated the number of children who have been detained at 30,000.

"'It might be a claw, for the flesh there is upon it,' was the Spirit's sorrowful reply. 'Look here.'"

A number of military bases are being used to house UACs. Fort Sill Army base in Lawton, OK will house 600. Lackland Air Force Base in San Antonio, TX is already near its capacity of 1,200.

"From the foldings of its robe, it brought forth two children; wretched, abject, frightful, hideous, miserable. They knelt down at its feet, and clung upon the outside of its garment."

Reports say another 94 non-military shelters are being used to house 6,218 UACs. HHS documents report housing at a government building in Baltimore, Maryland is planned.

"'Oh, Man, look here. Look, look down here,' exclaimed the Ghost."

U.S. immigration policy requires UACs to be placed in temporary shelters after which deportation proceedings will begin unless relatives or sponsors can be found to house them.

"They were a boy and a girl. Yellow, meager, ragged, scowling, wolfish; but prostrate, too, in their humility. Where graceful youth should have fulfilled their features out, and touched them with its freshest tints, a stale and shriveled hand, like that of age, had pinched, and twisted them, and pulled them into shreds. Where angels might have sat enthroned, devils lurked, and glared out menacing. No change, no degradation, no perversion of humanity in any grade, through all the mysteries of wonderful creation, has monsters half so horrible and dread."

WHY ARE THESE CHILDREN HERE?
"Scrooge startled back, appalled. Having them shown to him in this way he tried to say they were fine children, but the words choked themselves, rather than be parties to a lie of such enormous magnitude."

"'Spirit, are they yours?' Scrooge could say no more.

"'They are Man's,' said the Spirit, looking down upon them. 'And they cling to me, appealing from their fathers. This boy is Ignorance. This girl is Want. Beware them both, and all of their degree, but most of all beware this boy, for on his brow I see that written which is Doom, unless the writing be erased. Deny it,' cried the Spirit, stretching out his hand towards the city.

"'Slander those who tell it ye. Admit it for your factious purposes, and make it worse. And bide the end.'

"'Have they no refuge or resource?' cried Scrooge.

"'Are there no prisons?' said the Spirit, turning on him for the last time with his own words. ...The bell struck twelve."

ACCEPTANCE, OR A TWIST OF FATE

WHO AM I?

I am a college acceptance letter addressed to you that you found tucked away in your mother's desk 30 years after I was delivered. She never told you she had received me. Never mentioned me at all. It was a twist of fate you never knew about until after she had died and you were sorting things out. There, in the writing desk in her bedroom by her bed, along with the grade-school photos of cousins and old programs of musical concerts, lay one future for your life, an entire future in a single letter that went undelivered.

WHY AM I HERE?

She offered no excuse for why she never gave this letter to you. Your father was alive then, too. He must have known about my arrival as well. Of course he knew. I was from a religious college, one of the largest in the denomination of which HIS father, your GRAND-FATHER, was an ordained clergyman! You read your heartfelt cover letter to them both when you sent in your application. My response was to inform you that your heart's longing to pursue the path to becoming a minister of the denomination would be supported by the university (so long as you met requirements). You would be welcomed. Your life and career would merge onto the denomination's path and you would become part of the centuries-old stream like your grandfather. But, apparently that was NOT your fate.

WHAT DO I WANT?

Several roads meeting in the woods: some you are aware of, some you are not. Can we choose what we're FATED to be? No letter, no future. Remember, you were adopted at birth; that denominational connection was pure accident, anyway. Fate is capricious. It comes and it goes. Isn't it up to us to resolve the longings of our heart? Can we twist our fate? Didn't you resolve your longings and impulses for spirit and service? You didn't enter the church of the denomination but the church of the human spirit. Now I want to know which fate you accept today? Here? Now?

I AM YOUR CRISIS

WHO AM I?

I am the crisis that defines you. I may be that sudden automobile accident, that diagnosis, that unexpected email rejection. I can be as quick as a slap across the cheek. Or I may be one of those slow-moving crises that seems to eat away at your gut day after day. That step off the edge of the pool when you were 2 years old and went in over your head and gave you fear of water for the rest of your life. That poker game in which you were suddenly in way over your head. I am the panicky business investment which you have made and you're about to lose it all. The lie that came back to you. The little mistake that now has gotten out of control. Remember me? I took your beautiful watercolor painting and slopped indigo paint on it, trailed it across your pretty bright colors. I am the splash of indigo in your life: your heart attack, your cancer, the abortion, the perfect relationship gone wrong. There go your plans. Your hopes! Your dreams! Shot down in flames. And you are left with what? Broken dreams? Broken idealism? You're left broken.

WHY AM I HERE?

I bring you choices you would never make for yourself. I come to you, and your higher self offers your weaknesses up to me, just like Father Abraham. You are the son I must slay. I take you and I break you so you can have a choice. I give you choice, just like God gave Abraham that choice. I un-fix the fixed. I cause you to consider tightening up what's loosey-goosey. What will you do? Will you blot up the indigo paint on your pretty colors? Pretend I never happened?

Will you give up? Cry over your broken dreams? Get corrective surgery? How will you hide a broken heart? Get 'tude? Look for a White Knight? (You know, that indigo will never TOTALLY blot up! Everyone can tell. Everyone knows.) The memory will always be there.

Why were you broken? Was it something you did? Or something you ARE? Are you guilty? Have something to hide? Were you broken to let something OUT? Or to let something IN? Is being broken the end of something else? Or, is it only the beginning? How do you respond? How will your higher self respond?

Everyone starts with naïve idealism. But once you're broken you have the possibility to create achieved idealism out of the ashes of your dreams that went down in flames. "Achieved Idealism," a second marriage of you and your disillusioned self. It's discovery, recovery, learning and the lesson. You're not a pretty couple. A little indigo around the edges, imagination, deep, dark indigo, mixing with the crimson, yellow and blue, new hues appearing stronger, deeper, more powerful than you ever imagined. That's why I'm here. To create the new, improved and damaged you.

WHAT DO I WANT?
I want to live, and love, in universal imperfection. Couch surf with your karmic carpool. I am in the limbless arms of another who holds you. I am the ravaged face. The blind eyes. The drooping stroke smile. The limp. The drooling happy friend. I bring the impossible together with the improbable. I want you with me. I want you never to forget me, and I want you to carry me in your heart . . . right where Abraham was aiming the knife.

I AM THE MOTHER YOU NEVER MET

WHO AM I?

I am the mother you have always longed to know. The night you were conceived was a night filled with fireworks the way New Year's is always celebrated in San Antonio. I was 17 and I was a firecracker! I was at a party with some of the girls from TJ (Thomas Jefferson High School). There was a record player in a living room and all the furniture was piled on the front porch. We had to go outside to make out. The guys had booze in the trunks of their cars. I was with a guy I met who was a trainee at Lackland AFB.

At midnight he drove in a big old Plymouth way out on the north side, almost to Helotes! (He got lost.) I had him park on a hill so we could look at the lights. Didn't happen. We spent 5 minutes. All he wanted was what guys always want. He had to get out to take off his pants. He looked so white and skinny in the moonlight. It was cold when he came back in.

We lay on the Plymouth front seat. He held me but his legs were cold. My panties and my garter belt confused him in the dark. We warmed up as he fumbled around. The angles were awkward. I could hear firecrackers exploding. He was on me with weight and pressure. The windows fogged. I wiped a place on the passenger window and glimpsed a star overhead. That was my lucky star. Then the pushing got intense and I closed my eyes and I held him in.

WHAT DO I WANT?

I guess you would like me to say that I loved him. That, perhaps, he had given me a ring. That we had talked about getting married. It was New Year's Eve! It was a party! I was in high school. I wanted to belong to someone that night. He was nice. Quiet. Maybe you're quiet, too. I just let him happen inside me. I just let it happen. I guess a lot of things "just happened" in my life. But I kept you away from all that.

If you had a heartache because I gave you up for adoption, that was only ONE heartache. My gift to you was keeping you away from all the heartaches in MY life: a marriage way too young because I didn't know what to do when a boy gives you a ring; drunkenness, my parents' and his; the whole other set of kids I had with him; and then, my rage and HIS rage; divorce; bitterness; regret about you.

I wish you could tell me what you saw about me when you were in the spiritual world above that Plymouth. What did you see about me that made you want to pick me? Was there something you thought I was gonna do or be? Or could have been? What was it about me that caused you to pick me to be your mother? Why did you choose me?

WHY AM I HERE?

You were a spark that must have WANTED to catch hold in me. Why you wanted me to carry you, I don't know. Because the things that happened once you were in my belly were things that came from outside me. YOU must have brought it all together, because I couldn't have. The blood thing, for example. You got the AB type from your father and me. That's the rarest type of blood on earth. Then the Rh factor was very, very unusual, they said, and it made me sick and almost killed you in March. When they discovered all of that, then it was REALLY out of my hands.

Maybe I could have kept a normal baby if I could have had you at home or at my grandma's. But it got way out of hand. They took you six weeks early, in July, to save your life. They gave you blood transfusions and put you in an incubator. They wouldn't let me hold you.

The doctor knew the couple who adopted you. The woman picked the date he would induce labor and would be your birth date, because it was the birthday of her husband. On the one hand that seemed nice (you were her gift to her husband), but if you had been mine you would have been born under my lucky star I saw in the sky on New Year's Eve.

MY SOUL IS A SOCKEYE SALMON

WHO AM I?

I am an old guy swimming laps in the Community Therapy Pool, dodging the geriatrics with bathing caps in aqua-walkers and swimmees, avoiding the autistic teen in the Hawaiian-print suit who is screaming and leaping with delight. Three middle-aged regulars swim laps to emerge feeling younger and fitter. I admit my 45 minutes of laps seem to last a lifetime. I congratulate the bariatric woman for showing up.

My soul is a sockeye salmon and in its birth pool high above the Washington coast with its spawn-mates it leaps with youthful joy in the sweet water and circles and circles and then plunges downstream. It races over falls and leaps over obstacles until it reaches the salt water. My salmon soul adapts to the rigors of a huge cosmopolitan ocean-going social neighborhood. The toxic saline environment, which only a short time before would have killed it, now miraculously transforms it.

WHAT DO I WANT?

For many years I worked for a major corporation. Surviving there meant going with the flow, but you had to be able to change. You had to know how to handle the high and low tides of the marketplace. Timing was everything. A corporate rip tide downsizing can kill you. A competitive storm can slam you into rocks and cut you up. Avoid the sharks. I knew them but never trusted them. My salmon soul is more than middle-aged and weighs maybe 50 pounds. Its school has been living in the open sea for seven or eight years now, avoiding the sharks and seals. It navigates in the ocean by orienting itself with sunrise, sunset and major constellations of the northern hemisphere. It knows its age by seasons and by counting full moons.

I retired a few years ago. A 90-year-old woman and I have lapped one another for years now. She used to swim across open water following a row boat. I traveled in my car and made sales. Last night as my wife and I crossed the street to Sal's for pizza and wine I looked up and saw the belt of the constellation Orion. I remember how those stars still guide sailors. A vague fear arose that my salmon soul would someday soon feel compelled to return to its birth pool.

WHY AM I HERE?

My salmon soul cruises dangerously close to shore and near more predators like hawks, bears and men to test the mouths of creeks, searching for the route to the birth pool, listening to the sound of each river. It comes to one which makes the harmonics that sound familiar, like home. It turns in but finds fresh water. My salmon soul swims harder, urgently wishing to reach the warm pool of its life's end. It reaches the shallows and fertilizes eggs of a spectacularly beautiful dying female. My salmon soul feels the agony of the sweet water of death. But another soul will be born.

I stand in the shallows of the Community Therapy Pool. Around me are the dying, the geriatrics in their swimmees, the bariatric woman and me. We swim lap after lap on our way to where? To no cosmic purpose whatsoever? I find no comfort. How does a man find his way home, to his pool of death, let alone get there? I weep salty tears easily. I pull down my swim goggles and gasp for breath, as I can hardly can believe this is happening to me.

THE HEART: VALENTINE'S DAY 2014

WHO AM I?

"Some say the heart is just like a wheel, if you bend it, you just can't mend it." Some say the heart is just like the sun, brightly raying and enthusiastic. Some say the heart is just like a young girl doing cartwheels across the lawn on a spring evening. Some say the heart is just like a fist, clenched tight, pounding on the chest, ready to strike. Some say the heart is like an infant ready to be born, tender, vulnerable, open to the future. Some say the heart is like a prisoner in lock-down, in seclusion, shouting all night. Some say the heart is two halves, two palms outstretched to receive, open like an empty skull.

WHY IS THE HEART HERE?

Some say the heart is here to be a mechanical pump. Some say it is here to break and ache in youthful rawness. Some say the heart is the foot-warmer of the gods, to create naïve enthusiasm for the cold, cold heavens. Some say the heart is here to warm others with generosity. Some say the heart is here to touch and be touched with tenderness. Some say the heart is here to create joy, to hold the delicate place where all creativity begins.

Some say the heart is the place which knows rather than thinks. Some say the heart is predatory, cold, hard and lusting, the home of broken promises. Some say the heart bears our sorrows. Some say the heart is the place where our blood runs cold with fear and dread, the place of anger, rage, blame and retribution. The heart shows no mercy to the eyes.

WHAT DOES THE HEART WANT?

The heart wants to rhythmically give and take in what is called loving mutuality. The heart sends you on journeys which your brain never could have imagined. The heart weaves a web of mutuality to others, including your enemies. The heart wants the pride of ownership of your share of the world, but, once possessed, the heart seeks humility and wants you to guard against lust and vanity. In this way, the heart wants you to sacrifice yourself ruthlessly for yourself and for your brothers and sisters.

The heart wants you to experience the eternal moment between systole and diastole that is the doorway to the mystical.

THE SUBSTANCE OF LOVE

WHO AM I?

When I was growing up, maybe 3 years old, my family lived next door to an older "widow woman" with a bushy head of salt and pepper hair, who wore thick glasses, chain-smoked and laughed a deep, rumbly laugh. I called her Auntie Helen. She wasn't really my aunt, but in those days all the women on the block of tiny houses in our wannabe prosperous neighborhood in San Antonio were my aunts and all had full permission to act like my mother when my mother wasn't around. Many times I would go to Auntie Helen's house and the first thing she would ask is, "Have you eaten? Are you hungry?" and I would nearly always say, "No, I haven't eaten and yes, I am hungry." So Auntie Helen would cackle and prepare my favorite: Uncle Ben's "Instance" Rice with a big pat of butter. I remember Auntie Helen used a white enamel pan to boil the water and my mother didn't. I wondered if that was a magic pan that made the Instance rice taste better. It wasn't the rice that was special, it was what Auntie Helen put IN the rice: love. Auntie Helen transformed the Instance rice into the Substance of Love.

WHY AM I HERE?

Bees are a community of love. A hive is like a being. Individuals all selflessly devoted to gathering pollen in an extremely intimate fashion: parting the petals of the flower blossoms, crawling inside and licking, sucking and gathering the pollen. The bee then travels to another plant and, in that intimate visit, it pollinates that plant. Each hive is devoted to love and helping the flowers make love.

24

Imagine the hundreds of bees that live in each hive going out each day to make love to dozens if not hundreds of plants in a huge diameter around their hive. That's an amazing, invisible community task without which the flowers, fruits and plants in a large area cannot grow. They cannot pollinate themselves. I remember a Vacation Bible School song which goes, "Bees, Bees of Paradise, do the work of Jesus Christ. Do the work that no man can."

When the community bees return to the hive each day, they have a second intimate task: they transform the pollen into honey and propolis with which to feed the Queen and bee babies and make the hive secure. Honey, then, is made by a community devoted to love in order to serve the community. Rudolf Steiner called honey the "substance of love" and asks us to recall the inner experience of the taste of honey on our tongue. He says this is an experience of love. We all need to experience love.

WHAT DO I WANT?
Our world is going through a time where there are fewer resources and consequently people may individually feel needy for themselves but are actually rich in resources for one another, their community. Volunteering is better than bowling alone. I once spent a number of years teaching self-development courses as a volunteer in maximum security prisons. The men and I met as equals; we talked about life and I presented a few very simple but very challenging exercises from Rudolf Steiner. I'm not sure whose "self" was developed more, theirs or mine. So, if you can, volunteer at your church, hospital, Boys & Girls Club, weeding at a community farm, bussing tables at a food kitchen. Everybody can do something. Even calling an elderly neighbor and reminding them to take their medicine is an act of service, an act of love. Hunger of many types, physical and emotional, is on the rise in our communities. Become an Auntie Helen for someone else, transform your pan of Instance Rice into the Substance of Love.

ANOTHER WILLIE MAYS MIRACLE

WHO AM I?

I'm Brian's friend. Brian is dying. I know because he and I are in a cancer survivors' support group. He is dying of colorectal cancer. He was diagnosed about a year ago. We are both the same age, born in 1949. He was born in San Francisco and is Chinese American. I was adopted at birth. Since I don't know my birth mother or father, I told Brian I might be Chinese, too; and that maybe we're related. He laughed because I have no Chinese features and was born in Texas. What we do have in common is a love for baseball cards. I have a nearly completed '59 Topps set. And he has hundreds and hundreds of cards from the same vintage, too. But he loved my '59 Willie Mays card. We got together a couple of times to look at our cards and tell stories about being 10 years old and about the players we admired. He used to wait tables in his grandpa's restaurant in San Francisco so he could earn enough money to go watch the great Willie Mays play. Mays was his favorite player. Still is.

WHY AM I HERE?

Brian's wife called me and told me that Brian was dying. He was pretty close. She said that if I wanted to come and say good-bye I should probably come now. Going to a friend's death bed is an emotional thing. What will I say? What will we do? What does one do sitting at the death bed of a friend? I thought maybe he might want to say good-bye to Willie Mays, too; so I thought I'd take my '59 Topps Mays card. Maybe the card would give us something to talk about. My God, I thought, he will be so sedated because of the pain,

I thought a moment of joy might help. So I went to my card collection and took out my '59 Mays. The '59 Topps card is the one with the player photos in a circle. Mays' card is a solid yellow background. Mine was in a thick plastic screw-together case. I slipped it into my pocket and drove to the hospital, just a few miles away.

WHAT DO I WANT?

I went to Brian's room. His wife, Karen, greeted me, sobbing. I hugged her. She said that Brian was drifting in and out of consciousness but my being there would give her a moment to step out of the room. She clutched me and wept. I reached in my pocket and felt for Willie so that I could keep my composure. When she left, I walked to Brian's bed side and took out Willie.

"Brian! It's Jean," I said softly several times.

There was no response.

Then I whispered, "I brought Willie Mays."

There was a long pause and then he stirred. "...what?" he murmured softly from very far away.

I held up the card. "I brought my Willie Mays card."

His eyes opened slightly.

"Willie Mays?" he whispered incredulously.

We went back and forth like this for a long time until he returned from the angelic realm and regained some earthly consciousness. Finally he pushed himself up on his pillow and asked, "Where's my glasses?"

I handed him his glasses and he put them on and looked at the card. He gazed at it adoringly and then he looked over at me.

And then, as so frequently happens in loving relationships between friends and lovers, the Angelic Being of Humor spread his wings over us:

"Are you *giving* me your '59 Willie Mays?" he said looking over at me.

"Are you *kidding*?" I asked. "Nice try. No way."

"Okay." He smiled. "I'll just hold it."

Then he talked about seeing the great Willie Mays until he got tired again and lay back down and went to sleep. The warmth of the Being of Humor stayed with us for the remaining time we had together. I made sure the card was in my pocket when I left.

I AM THE BEING OF QUIET, AND YOU ARE NERVOUS? ANXIOUS? OVERWHELMED?

WHO AM I?

Hi! How you doin'? I'm Quiet. Remember me? Long time no see. You've been BUSY! Me? Oh, hanging out. When was the last time we got together? Oh, go ahead, answer that. Yeah, I know, cell phones, what're ya gonna do? Man, you got a lot of demands on your time. Still married? How's the wife? Girlfriend? How many kids you got now? How many jobs you work? And the wife? Oh, that's okay, send the text. I'll wait. Look at that! You got a big-screen TV with over 200 channels. Man, that's GREAT. Loaded iPod. Kindle. You're IMPORTANT! You got bills to pay. Lots of bills. So how's it going with that little issue you wanted to talk with me about? What'd you call it? "Nervous gut"? You said you were feeling driven. Overwhelmed. Anxious. Couldn't sleep. What was that you said about "aimless searching"? Forgetfulness? Oh, you go ahead and take that call, it may be important, they're all important. How to find inner strength?

WHAT DO I WANT?

Quiet is the super-structure under your thinking and feelings. If you can't think and your feelings get all crossed up, life gets crazy. Quiet is the George Washington Bridge to your heart, but with three lanes closed down it's a disaster. What's up with you filling your so-called "free time" with technology? That ain't gonna get you where you want to go faster! Just how many computing devices does one person need? You have a smart phone, a laptop, a game box, a desktop computer, wide-WIDE-screen TV, cable/Internet service, Netgear, and when you happen to be in a place where you can't get Wi-Fi or your laptop can't get online, you always carry an assortment of small single-purpose handheld games. When you're at work, you're constantly on the phone texting, e-mailing, Facebooking, and on and on. So what happens when three lanes out of five lanes of your life are closed down? All of those other activities pile up on the only two lanes available. Which means? Jammed up! Anxious? Doh-oh!?

WHY AM I HERE?
Take your fingers off the keyboard and put your cell phone down. Put the palms of your hands together. See that little gap down the middle? Yeah, between your hands. That's where Quiet lives in your life. That's all the space you give me! Your left hand is "cause," your right hand is "effect." That's the gap between "cause" and "effect" or stimulus and response. It is not much of a gap but it's all you need to be human and not to be totally automatic like a computer. That's enough time to PAUSE. To STOP. To GRAB HOLD of the situation. To WAIT a moment before you respond to that call, text, or electronic DEMAND. How about you let the phone ring while you count to three because you're in control. Make mini-moments of Quiet. That's also what you would call your RESOLVE. That's the space you need to get into to find Quiet and not be buffeted by your inner aimless searching and the outer demands the world. That's where your true self sits, right there in that little space between your two palms. Now it's up to you how you use your hands.

THE MIDNIGHT SHIFT

WHO AM I?

I work the midnight shift from 10 p.m. to 2 a.m. or some other ungodly hours. I may work the dimly lit warehouse, the brightly lit manufacturing shop floor, the color-balanced print shop, loading trucks, unloading trucks, sorting, boxing, feeding parts into the machine or whatever repetitive task is required to keep the shift work going in Cuautitlan, Kathmandu, Sao Paulo, Dusseldorf, Detroit or wherever. It's pretty much the same repetitive, soul-numbing work. Or worse, it could be something like telemarketing: cold-calling, 98% rejection, which is hard not to take personally. Mostly to get through the shift I had to build a shell, wear a mask, mentally put on armor, or create a persona, certainly split my inner life from my outer job. It's called the gap in the soul. It can happen with ANY job, even white-collar jobs and service jobs. It becomes a real problem when the protective sheath gets too hard or fixed and is something you can't escape from or get out of and you get stuck. It can happen. You can see it sometimes.

WHY AM I HERE?

We are all cogs in the worldwide economic machine. We all play our parts: consumers, manufacturers, service providers, employees, everyone. We trade our energy and human resources to do a specific part of a larger process which goes on and on somewhere else. I take boxes from a giant conveyor belt and load them into trailers which go to another warehouse where they are unloaded and re-loaded into other trucks which then go to another warehouse on the next leg of the delivery process. I am in Texas and even at midnight it is sometimes well over 100 degrees F in the trailer I am loading. I munch salt tablets and drink water but still I get leg cramps. High overhead is a steel grate. I see guys sorting the boxes onto five conveyor belts. They stand under giant fans. I ask my supervisor how do I get the job under the fans? "Memorize this," he says and hands me a small booklet with the names of hundreds of cities in Texas and their zip codes and dozens of small towns surrounding each city. They are broken into five regional sort centers. "Be able to look at a box, see the zip code and put it on the appropriate belt with 98% accuracy."

Wow! Now that's a challenge. Suddenly my job got interesting, and interesting engages the ego.

WHAT DO I WHAT?

I want to be under the fans. So I research, find a special memory trick called the link and, after some hard work, I memorize the zip codes and pass the test. Everybody who works any midnight shift work does something to meet the challenge of their situation. Either you become the shell, the mask, the numbed zombie, the automaton or you find an inner creative game to play that nourishes your soul. I used the link and played with the link. When I became a sorter, I used to stand next to a guy named Gary who would laugh all shift long. I asked him once what he laughed about and he said, "I'm making movies in my mind." I'll bet.

I used to wonder about the people who were going to receive the package I sorted and whether or not they had tried to overcome the repetitiveness of their own lives. Or ever tried to get beyond the shells and masks they created? Or ever once thought that there was somebody like me on a midnight shift somewhere who made it possible for them to get that package? Or glued the soles on their running shoes in China? Or made their batteries in Mexico? It's a shift when you can think through any day-to-day economic transaction and go all the way to the source of the product.

I AM YOUR HANDS

WHO AM I?

I am your hands. At play. At work. Folded. Cupped. Applauding. Busy. Patting. Caressing. Touching. Tenderly exploring. Smacking. Crushing. Tickling. Pushing. Ges-tur-ing! Thumbing. Picking. Applauding. Fondling. Entwining. Knitting. Sewing. Playing an instrument. Smoothing. Soothing. Questioning, why? Why!? Saying stay! Sit. Come. Fists punching. Slapping! Loading. Saluting. Waving. Preserving. Defending. Gripping. Clutching. Pointing. Fingering! Snapping, ah-ha! That's it! Plucking. Buttoning. Zipping. Hitchhiking. Texting. Dialing. Agile and extraordinary. Eyes of the soul. Reverent. Knitting a veil for the Queen of Heaven. Making the Sign of the Cross. Flipping off an aggressor. Covering your mouth in surprise! The point of contact for formative forces. Forces of science, music, craft, the arts, mechanics, technology, and love. The hands are all about love. Touching and being touched.

WHY AM I HERE?

It is the Norns (female beings) who weave the threads of destiny for you in Norse mythology. In Greek mythology it is Ariadne who hands you the thread to find your way out of the labyrinth and avoid your sacrificial death. In your own hands is the red thread that runs through every event of your life from what you once were to what you have become onward to what you will become. Your hands are the keeper of the threads of the loom of your life, be they colorful threads of persons, places, activities and things or of your electronic loom, which leads you on through threaded messages. As the saying goes, these threads of your fate are in our own hands.

WHAT DO I WANT?

The poet Robert Browning wrote, "Ah, but a man's reach should exceed his grasp, or what's a heaven for?" What is it that our hands want? Of all the actions which our hands can take, it is perhaps reaching that may be one of the most significant. What are your hands reaching for?

SHE COAXES THE HUMAN SPIRIT

WHO IS SHE?
She is MD, therapist, mother, but in the pre-scientific era she would have been the Hermit in her cave or the Wise Woman in front of the fire. Today the fire into which she gazes is a medical records computer screen. She is the Oracle who consults her runes, the bones, the stars, the history, the lab results, her notes and her heart. She turns her prophetic gaze inward on herself and recalls the patient's rattling chest, the general strength or weakness, fever, and clammy touch. She sees each prior check-up and looks into her mind's eye and sees us, her patients, in detail. She fields a call from her daughter and discusses their dinner plans. Then she adjusts herself inwardly and comes to the exam room.

WHY IS SHE HERE?
She walks through offices, ERs, waiting rooms, quiet or noisy, dressed in her white lab coat. She pauses at the doorknob to the exam room and rallies her weariness into a sense organ which she will focus on the patient. There is nothing that passes this good woman's eye. Nothing too trivial for her to consider. She will take in each of us and compare it mentally with her inner review, looking for changes. In this wounded world, the quiet power of her eye and her stern gaze gives comfort to the frightened, courage to the dying, and careful attention to the Willy Lomans who whine and carp about declining forces, failure or change.

WHAT DOES SHE WANT?

In her childhood days she coaxed frogs into jars and yellow perch onto hooks. Her patients too are wild things and shy. Some put on brave faces. Others seek sympathy. Some angrily deny their fate. The exam room reeks of regret. Holding powerful emotions and great science on some unseen scale of destiny, she seeks to coax the human spirit in each patient into full flame. She starts with small questions, "How are you today?" and listens. Agonizingly slow she can hear the heart creaking open or if the human thing is unable to arise, she is prepared to retire in hope, pain, fear or grief in her solitude.

ENTER THE TIMEKEEPER

WHO AM I?

I am the Timekeeper. I am the one who divides your life into segments and those segments into segments. I am an active agent in your soul. I am the deadline, the due date, the thin veneer of control which efficient management desires. You must obey, otherwise your accomplishment, no matter how skillfully executed, is flawed because it was late. Timing is everything. We started early, you and me. Remember elementary school? Three tardies equals an absence.

Don't you judge your life on someone else's timeline? Of course you do! Start times, quitting time, lunch time, dinner time, time off, clock in, clock out. And, generally aren't you too young? Too old? Too early? Too late? An extra day off? No way! What IS your life expectancy? How many days until Christmas? We build prisons based on reading scores of pre-K kids knowing they are already too late to EVER catch up. We grant abortions based on fetus age. The Timekeeper carves up of your life, your soul, society and the earth.

WHY AM I HERE?

Progress and efficiency created me in the 1800s, when technology began its ascent. There is no progress without me, no efficiency. I am the orderly, the economic, the bureaucratic, the manageable, the bell curve and the algorithm. I am physically essential for geo-synchronous satellites and time zones. I link your cell phone or tablet to every machine and every technology on earth. I am technology, and technology is not possible without me!

I timekeep you. All this control is about freedom. Once the moon and the sun ruled your soul, and your entire life was owned by those two orbs. Now the Timekeeper and technology give you freedom from a life driven by sunrise and sunset. Remember labor-saving devices? Timesaving devices. I am the TimeKEEPER, remember? But do I keep time FOR you? Or FROM you?

WHAT DO I WANT?

I advise you not to step out into nature. Out there is a natural world not under my control: sun and moon, day and night, full moons and new moons, equinoxes and solstices. Seasons! But you, YOU are FREE from these inconveniences, aren't you? So what if the cold and flu season is directly connected with the autumnal solstice and the waning of the light!? So what if circadian rhythms within your body are vital to your health? You can ignore them. What's a little stress? Nothing that a pharmaceutical can't fix, eh? Who are you going to believe? Nature and your body? Or the Timekeeper? Remember, I AM scientific.

WHAT FEEDS US

WHO AM I?

I am what feeds us in the food, what nourishes us, what offers health. I'm the secret ingredient that is no ingredient at all. I am more than minerals, fiber, proteins, and fats. I give the soil health and life through the agency of microbes, worms, and unseen living things. I give the seeds to those who, using ancient wisdom, care for their vitality and distribution across the world. I'm the freedom of the animals on the farm and the wild things that are there also. I'm the warmth and joy of the sun, weaving the seasons, the days and weeks. I am the air we breathe and the weather. I am the rhythms of the moon and the loom of sun, moon and stars of the night. I am the intricate, vast network of roots, water tables, creeks, streams, rivers, man-made dams and rain that connect each farm to us all. I am the tending, the weeding, the organization, care, and husbandry of the farmer and farm workers. The community gardens, the CSA farms, the neighbors breaking bread in meals that daily roll around the earth, time zone after time zone.

WHY AM I HERE?

The food is lacking without your enjoyment. I am the mother who works hard to see her family is nourished with love. I am the chef who studies the arts and sciences of taste and beauty to enrich your experience. I am your tongue which can tell and your nose which knows and your eyes which light up with delight at the extraordinary quality your artistry adds. I am the vintner whose love of terroir gives us the genius of another living being. I feed your skin and hair with beauty, oils and aromas that lift your soul. I am the doctors and pharmacists whose medicines harmonize your well-being. I am your sense of language to describe good things even with a simple "m-m-m-m!" You are an essential part of the food chain so eat! And when you are done, do not waste what is left. Lovingly returned to soil, compost will feed the insects, animals, microbes and earth to transform the food chain into a community.

WHAT DO I WANT?

Why do humans not lovingly nourish one another? Amid your abundance, how can you send one another to bed hungry? I want the goodness of your soul to be reflected in the goodness of the soil. I am what makes you human and I am what make the humus. I want the freshness and beauty of the first day of creation to be reflected in what goes on your table. I am what feeds you in the food. Children, feed one another! I am that I am. You are my hands and feet.

THIS THING BETWEEN US

WHO AM I?

It is this thing between us. Something we wrestle with all the time. This thing between us is something about me, about what I used to be. It's my fault. We don't talk about it. We use polite words, small words. I get tired just trying to carry it, but I'm afraid that if I let go it will sink into forgetfulness and won't ever go away. It can't. Your father sees it. He said, "You brought him home. You promised him. You deal with him." And your mouth gets grim. We go to bed but we don't touch. I try to please you but feel I have let you down somehow. I can't be good enough. Do I have to atone for something that I used to be? I don't know. This thing between us, this silent thing, is turning into something else. I can see it gaining energy in your violent indifference.

WHY AM I HERE?

We had an agreement and I gave you your heart's desire. And now I'm here and we are alone together. Now I just can't look up. I bear it all. I stuff it. I zip it. I watch your up-tilted nose and grim mouth. I am a sponge for your continual disdain. I have become cold blooded to adjust to the chill that is always between us. I have a collection of moments that should have been tender and warm but weren't. How can we hold hands if yours are clenched fists? You don't suffer in silence. You've built a wall between us brick by brick with put downs and shut downs.

WHAT DO I WANT?

You play the perfect princess and that means the ugly thing between us is me, the frog in the fairy tale. This story is about to turn violent, very violent. So be it. I prefer hot violence to cold. You will throw me with all your might against the wall of your cold-hearted indifference, hoping that I will shatter and be transformed into a handsome prince. I can only hope the act of violence that releases me will soften your heart and you will be able to love me. No... No! This thing between us has been an illusion! Oh, God! Help me become dis-illusioned.

I AM DARWIN'S BRAIN

WHO AM I?

I am Darwin's brain. It was I who had phenomenal insights. Everyone said I was brilliant, a genius! That's true. And I should know. I am Sir Charles Darwin's brain. Is it because I am so uniquely designed that I am so special? Well, partially. When I was a child, I played freely in nature. Then, up until the age of 30, I had Sir Charles feed me a steady diet of poetry and art and music! Each week we painted, attended concerts and galleries! And read SHAKESPEARE! It was glorious. And jokes! Lots of jokes and laughter.... Anything to nourish me and get me thinking in different fashions. This prepared me for releasing my genius. Who knew about neuron theory? But I nourished Sir Charles' neurons, so I was like the young Muhammad Ali of gray matter: lithe and quick and ready to get into the ring with science!

WHY AM I HERE?

Habit! Blessed, habit! Habits of thinking. Narrow minded doing what you're good at over and over is a habit! I hurt myself. Repetitive thinking injury. The professional demands were fierce. Sir Charles has only fed me facts and data, facts and data, FACTS AND DATA for MANY years! Forced me to grind out General Laws, and for General Laws you need LOTS of facts and data. I was forced to crunch the numbers, grind out the laws like a machine that grinds sausage. I believe that such a steady diet of habitual thinking has pumped up certain neural pathways while other parts of me have atrophied! Darwin's brain has atrophied because of a conceptual, perceptual habit of thinking. Who would have thought? I certainly didn't, and I'm Darwin's brain!

WHAT DO I WANT?

Joy! Freedom! To feel my toes in the grass like a kid again! Parts of me are GONE, I tell you! Simply gone. The other day I rummaged through some neurons and realized, Darwin's brain realizing, can you imagine, that my capacity to think, REALLY THINK, is now limited to only certain types of thoughts?! Love, my feeling life, I've misplaced it. And has anyone seen Darwin's morality? I hope it's here someplace under facts and data! I once read poetry each week, now it makes me nauseous, especially Shakespeare. I've enfeebled myself through disuse. Look, if you gotta make sausage, mix things up! Don't just make horsemeat sausage, make rabbit sausage! Use 50% horsemeat and 50% rabbit: one rabbit to one horse. You're not laughing. That's a statistician's joke. Geez, Darwin's brain has lost it.

AGE 28-30: THE WISER PERSON WITHIN US

WHO AM I?

The wiser person within us watches while we are riding the wave of our 20s, a time during which we feel we can do ANYTHING. This feeling is true because for many, the early 20s may be under the influence of others: parents, family, school, sports, or other activities surrounding natural abilities with which we have been born and which we are encouraged to pursue.

By about age 28 many people reach the limit of this world. We can feel these capacities begin to diminish, or we grow jaded and we sense we need a new direction in which to grow. This is when the wiser person within us brings our limitations or our personal shortcomings to meet the demands of our future destiny in order to help us prepare to become.

In many biographies, this prompts a crisis that happens at about age 28. This is called the crisis of talent. Will we find a source of renewal of our gifts and natural abilities from the past? Or do we feel compelled, even driven, to break out and attempt to radically change ourselves?

WHAT DO I WANT?

When I was 28, I had spent many years in printing/publishing. But I had a dream of becoming a writer. My wiser person within used my boss as my excuse for me to quit and prompt my crisis of talent.

My wife was working and so she agreed to support us for one year while I became a writer.

My crisis deepened because the wiser person within me knew that I would fail. It is impossible to become a professional writer in one year! But this helped me confirm the truth of the world. I tried. I wrote a novel, I wrote a screenplay, I wrote for neighborhood and alternative newspapers. But I wrote nothing for which anyone would pay me. It was clear, after my year, I would not be able to earn a living as a writer. I was too proud to go back to printing/publishing. My wife and the wiser person within me said: "Go get a job."

Then the wiser person within me helped me realize that it wasn't the writing craft that needed all the attention, it was the BEING ME part that needed to change. (Uh-oh!)

WHY AM I HERE?

After the crisis of talent, a deeper phase shift may be necessary, as it was in my case. I would never achieve the outer goal of being a successful writer unless I changed inwardly: dealt with my pride and anger, and gained some humility and social skills while polishing my natural writing skills. And more.

On the inside the seed of what you wish to become has been planted. But the seed of your future lies within the hard shell of who you are. In my case, I had done a great job of building up this cynical, opinionated, arrogant guy. All this had to be dissolved before the new and improved me could emerge and take root. That dissolving is terribly painful but absolutely necessary to allow the future to sprout.

In my case, being humbled was solvent for my hardened ego. I took any job I could to meet the responsibilities of family. Once I began to soften, I noticed that my wife and some of her friends were seeking a spiritual path. Was I even aware there was a path? No. I had all the answers there, too. So the wiser person woke me up to lots of things that were hardened into answers. The wiser person opened an inner space that became filled with questions: Was there something more that I ought to strive for beyond a profession (what I "profess" or say I want to be)? Was there in any sense a calling, something coming from outside leading me into the future?

The more I changed, the more it was possible for me to change and the more the wiser person within me was able to lead.

I AM AN INMATE IN MY MARRIAGE, FAMILY AND JOB

WHO AM I?

I am a volunteer at a maximum security prison in Jackson, Michigan. For ten years I have been teaching a weekly course designed to give my students greater inner freedom through self-control. After I put my belongings in a locker, I'm wanded, go through the metal detector, and I'm issued a panic alarm for my belt. Then the 1-inch-thick iron gate rolls shut behind me and I am within an atmosphere of power and a technology of control. I have signed away my freedom while I am inside. I am under the control of the system. I must do as they direct. This is not anonymous power. Once while attempting to gain entry to a class in a prison in Pennsylvania, because of mistaken identity, I was strip searched. If you teach "self-control" one must be able to practice what you teach.

WHY AM I HERE?

There is no obligation for inmates to attend my class. No college credits. I am a volunteer and unpaid. There are no rewards for attending. In a sphere of control and power, where men earn time off for good behavior or must attend court-stipulated programs about addiction, anger management, and so forth, they choose my class freely. Some think it will be entertaining, but it's not. It's a ten-week course and, by the end, only about 25% of the original enrollees remain. The exercises are simple, but self-control means controlling your responses to outer pressures and impulses from within. It takes a lot of practice. The exercises were created by Rudolf Steiner: control of feelings, control of thinking, control of will (or equanimity), positivity, open mindedness and then balancing all five at the same time.

I teach this course because I practice along with the inmates. After all, I am an inmate in my own self-created power systems: marriage, a family and a job. And I live in our modern, "free" society.

WHAT DO I WANT?
This is an age of power. But every age has its own Medusas of power who attempt to control the hearts and minds of men.

Anonymous power in media and technology is every bit equal to the power of prison walls. Satellites whiz overhead and create an unseen and unknown net around us for purposes of control that we can't even imagine.

And we who are not behind walls are impulsive. We may be too quick to give away our freedom when we hear the words "I love you," and find ourselves held captive in abusive relationships.

And men and women sadly give up their freedom, their fortune, their families and their lives for heroin or other addictive drugs, liquor, or cigarettes. My state, Vermont, now has an epidemic of babies being born who are addicted to heroin and not by their choice.

Viktor Frankl survived the Nazi concentration camps and discovered a place of freedom in the human soul, a place of personal power in which we all can be free. The men I met in prison began to rediscover their power through self-control, but, as I said, it takes a little practice. They also discovered one another, and a little dose of community gave them encouragement and hope. Perhaps the second secret about overcoming power and finding freedom is community. That takes practice, too. And a whole lot of self-control.

I AM DIS-INCARNATION:
AGE 42, THE HINGE YEAR

WHO AM I?

I am dis-incarnation, the gradual grapevine step that you do as you dance your way off the stage of life. I've been in the script for years; you're only just now beginning to notice my entrance. Perhaps it was the wrinkles. Maybe a little arthritis around the edges. Some hair loss, mmm? White hairs? And the menopause ads seem more present.

Your vitality and health, which all these years lived deep in your skeleton, is now packing up and going to Florida. All your hormonal doo-dads are beginning to pack their bags, too. They know you are watching the commercials that suggest that their sell–by date is approaching. They will be replaced by hormonal treatments as offered by the young, virile and buxom sales team on the telly. Truthfully, with the exception of big-time pharma for men with E.D., this is the same stuff that's been offered since the late 1800s to generation after generation. You do age. You will die. Still, spending money and applying creams will give you and me something to do and pass the time while you dis-incarnate!

WHY AM I HERE?

Ah, but this is an EXCITING time! Around age 42 is THE hinge year. You may feel it's too late! Or you're getting bogged down. Or strangely liberated. At age 42 you can look into the windshield of your life and see the off-ramp for death. And out the rearview mirror, your birth and childhood waving bye-bye! This is like the autumnal equinox of your life, in which the future and the past are in balance. Some say it feels as if you have a moment of weightlessness, in which all forces are equal; that can be frightening. Others say that you can feel the greatest sense of freedom and potential.

About age 42 is the year in many biographies in which break-throughs and radical shifts of all kinds have taken place: Galileo made his first telescopic discoveries; Freud published *Studies on Hysteria*; it was Jung's most critical period; Betty Friedan published *The Feminine Mystique*; and Rosa Parks chose to stay seated.

WHAT DO I WANT?

This mountaintop experience is a great time to look at your life. Your child-rearing years may be behind you, but now is the time for spiritual children. And a new type of seeing may be possible; an inner vision may bring you insights that you will learn to trust.

But now is the time for you to make serious plans and do research for how you will spend your life after age 62, the next great hinge!

To rephrase an old saying that says:

"From age 21 to age 42 we try many things and learn how to live.

"From age 42 to age 63 we learn to sort through what we have lived and choose what we love.

"From age 63 to death, we live only what we love."

LISTEN AS MR. BALLOON SUSPENDS DOUBT LIKE COGNITIVE KRYPTONITE

Listen to the Mr. Balloon commercial at: www.the-three.com

WHO AM I?

"Hi Boopie! Mr. Balloon here!"[1] I'm a cute and seemingly harmless radio puppet created in the mid 1980s for a c-store client. Despite the reality of your local c-store: dirty floors, a clerk who can't speak English, and overpriced products, Mr. Balloon suspends doubt like cognitive kryptonite.

Creating funny ads is a serious business. The title of my Master's thesis was: "The Use of Comedy in Radio Advertising to Overcome Cognitive Dissonance." In simple English this means my research was going to test whether or not radio comedy ads can help overcome doubt and cause audiences to buy stuff. I never finished the thesis because I was busy writing radio comedy ads and selling lots of stuff for major corporations, no analytical research required.

WHY AM I HERE?

You should know why radio comedy advertising is so effective. The basic speaking-listening communication phenomenon goes something like this: you listen to me and you get into the flow of what I say, and your critical thinking dims a bit. Essentially, you go to sleep. Radio reduces your focus to only the audio, so you get even more tuned in. And sound effects focus your attention even more. The only way you stay conscious at all is because you create some sort of antisocial force within yourself. This critical thinking is a type of cognitive dissonance or doubt. You may say, "Cute commercial, but my local c-store, ooo!" Mr. Balloon's job is to leave you with a DIFFERENT emotion that will erase those critical feelings: a warm smile!

WHAT DO I WANT?

Advertisers spend thousands of dollars to sell their products. A part of the process is overcoming your natural cognitive dissonance. Why not strengthen your capacity for independent thinking?

Let's take this little test. Let's use this Mr. Balloon commercial to learn something: Play it again and I invite you to drag your critical thinking back from wherever it went when you began to enjoy Mr. Balloon, and be a bit analytical about the commercial

Each market situation requires the right type of advertising to sell the product. So each commercial has certain things which the client requires for the commercial: product name, price, sponsor name, etc. The clever ad writer has to meet these requirements AND enable Mr. Balloon to be kryptonite to your critical thinking. After you hear the spot again, ask yourself these simple questions: What products were named? How many times was the product named? And how many times was the c-store named? And how easy or difficult was it to stay conscious?

Have fun, Boopie!

Jean Yeager is an award winning radio comedy advertising writer and producer. Hear other radio comedy ads at his web site:
http://www.the-three.com

I AM YOUR MASK

WHO AM I?

I am your mask. Inside me is the other person you're working on becoming: the imperfect but REAL you. Inside your mask is your true character. Or so you hope. You went with that common advice: fake it until you make it. So I am what you think people want to see that you are: the really good wife and mother, the professional woman, the student, the attentive and caring father, the nice neighbor, or some kind of pretentious, holier-than-thou religious moralist that buys you cred with those folks on the outside you want to impress. I may be the work mask, the church or religion mask. The guy/gal-pal mask. The volunteer service mask. Keeping all this straight takes a lot of energy, more energy than being truthful, being who you really are. And then there is the problem of getting caught in your mask forever, forgetting to spend time building the REAL you so that at the end of the day all you have is a really strong mask and your soft, or empty, middle.

WHY AM I HERE?

I am here to put you under pressure. True character is revealed through decisions under pressure. Your true character, the one inside, is built out of actions, mistakes, attempts and learning. Risk taking. The icon painters talk about an outer icon, which is the art object, and the inner icon, which is formed by the icon-making process. The inner icon is within the artist and is made by putting your character under pressure, confronting yourself through the process: fear of not being good enough, of being imperfect with the paint. Well, you can imagine. It's the opposite of faking it: being truthful. Risking being new, immature, imperfect, and revealing this to others, no masks. So if you go through life faking courage, and not taking the occasion to practice genuine courage, when will you ever have the courage to really be courageous? When will you feel the exquisite inner struggle of self-confrontation? Or honesty? Or selflessness (there's one that takes practice).

WHAT DO I WANT?

I have all the courage in the world, so it is easy for your mask to tell you what to do. Maybe that's the way it is for others who tell you what to do. So here's what I WANT: I want you to put something meaningful for you but insignificant for anyone else in your pocket today. Got that? Something insignificant: a pen, a paperclip, anything, but YOU give it meaning. This object is your reminder that you WILL practice courage. When you touch it, you will remember that only YOU can build the one inside. The next step is the action step: you will DO something small but courageous. This is not for ME! I'm your MASK! Do it for YOU, the one inside. The imperfect one. The one only you know about. You know who I mean. Then, tell no one you are doing this. Ever.

I AM THE TONGUE OF THE LIAR

WHO AM I?

I am the tongue of the liar and I am the best in the business. Some say our lineage goes back to the snake who lied about the Tree of Knowledge of Good and Evil. If I were to say that's a lie!, then you could count on it. God looks to our lineage to deliver and since then we have lied for and against just about everything. Every clan, tribe, country, religion and corporation needs an experienced tongue now and then. Who do you think is in the President's mouth from time to time? How about this one: "Weapons of mass destruction." At the U.N.! Or "Too big to fail." You see, it's not the lie, it's the tongue of the liar. It's how it rolls off the tongue that makes the difference. Everybody knew W and the Fed were lying; there was no doubt. What saved the day was the tongue that told those MONSTROUS, IMPOSSIBLE lies. Not every tongue can rise to the level of the impossible when needed. It's a gift.

WHY AM I HERE?

It's a great era to be the tongue of a liar! A Golden Age. An age of massive lies. Do we doubt genocide and global warming? Every day I make the rounds of the news outlets, like a mall, right? Some carry one kind of story. Another set of outlets carry the opposite. My guy surrounds himself with small minds so they can't deliver the big messages. That's MY job, to bring the BIG DEAL. My guy starts an interview and he smiles and pauses, he's on the launch pad with one easy softball question, like he's actually thinking (as if), and suddenly I'm running down this narrow mental alleyway between what is and what is not and he's caring nothing for his reputation or the international repercussions. Then I realize we have to totally change the game, tell the GRAND LIE, a GENERATIONAL lie! A lie so large and so all encompassing that it takes in the last 50 years of history about a specific topic and flips it on its head. The lie is so outrageous that they don't respond, they just report. Said often enough and with sincerity, the GRAND LIE is not a negative.

WHAT DO I WANT?
Besides the BIG lies that move countries and generations, I like the intimate lie, the lover's lie, the leader's lie. Sweet lies about glory, your glory. Those earnest looks and whispered promises. The touching, the hand shake held for a few moments longer than necessary, to show intention. The shoulder touch. I tell you that he knows what you want. He's listened to you. You're not alone. He's here for you, protecting you. The direct one-on-one eye contact. The motivating word from his mouth, a great-looking mouth. I tell you this will be dangerous, very dangerous. We won't let this fail, but it will take YOUR effort. You're so close you watch his mouth, watch the words roll off me and his determined chin. He's a person of flesh and blood and I tell you he's relying on you; we're ALL relying on you. He smells good and your nose wouldn't lie about a thing like that. His heart beats good and pure, like your heart. You believe him. You will do as he asks, even though it is very, VERY dangerous "...and you may lose your life. But the cause is worth it," says the tongue of the liar, quoting my ancestor, the snake.

I AM GALILEO AND SOCIAL MEDIA IS MY TELESCOPE

WHO AM I?

I am Galileo and social media is my telescope. I have been observing the relationship of the various spheres in the constellation of your social life through my telescope. These consist of three spheres of what has been a citizen-centric society: the economic sphere, the spiritual/cultural sphere and the rights/political sphere.

Each of these spheres has been presumed to revolve around the individual citizen (hence citizen-centric) and be governed by a specific ideal, virtue or principle. The spiritual/cultural sphere is governed by liberty or freedom: freedom to worship, study, learn, and follow the arts; the rights/political sphere is governed by equality: all are equal under the law; and the economic sphere is governed by brotherhood, the producer and consumer in a mutual relationship.

I have been watching these spheres through the social media telescope by which I see the vast comings and goings of behaviors, ideas and concerns of your citizenry.

I have concluded that you have been under a significant mis-apprehension! Things are NOT as they seem. The individual citizen is NOT the center of your society any longer. Your citizen-centric society has been an ILLUSION caused by geometry! There is a new and larger entity that influences all the other spheres. This discovery explains why certain things are not as they seem to you and why others have gone so wrong!

WHY AM I HERE?

My telescope shows that the three spheres which you once thought revolved around the individual citizen actually revolve around other more influential bodies: corporations. Corporations are the new center of your social heaven! Your society is now corporate-centric! In the 1600s I proved that the earth revolves around the sun. This is analogous. Corporations are larger than individual citizens, command more power and take more resources. They exert so much power, in fact, that they have changed the virtues or principles by which the spheres of your society operate!

Here is how the values have been changed:

SPHERE: WAS GOVERNED BY:
Economics: Brotherhood
Spiritual/Cultural: Freedom
Rights/Politics: Equality

SPHERE: NOW GOVERNED BY:
Economics: Liberty
Spiritual/Cultural: Equality
Rights/Politics: Brotherhood

These value shifts have had huge consequences for life as you knew it.

Economics: Corporations behave with total economic liberty and freedom to maximize profits (plunder, some say). There has been little or no regard for brotherhood. The rights sphere is set up to promote and protect this economic freedom!

Rights: No longer practicing equality. Representatives are being owned. Corporations and government act like a brotherhood and watch out for one another. Paid lobbyists write laws. State agencies spy using corporate data. Corporations are granted the rights of citizens. Watchdogs are now lapdogs. The military is now focused on protecting American corporate interests worldwide.

Spiritual/cultural: Free education? Now the state is in control through heavy subsidies directed by the state. Budgets are low and general education underfunded. State colleges, originally created with citizen money, now do research to benefit corporations, who then make citizens pay for those advances created at what were once their colleges.

I have checked my results by viewing your society through other telescopes: broadcast radio and television, cable media and print. I find the same result. You have a corporate-centric society and not a citizen-centric one. You might want to stop pretending it is otherwise. The world is NOT flat.

WHAT DO I WANT?

The last time I made some observations suggesting that the world was heliocentric and not geocentric, it did not go well. As if it was something I did! But (sigh) observation is observation and science is science and I AM Galileo!

The shift in values or principles I see in my social media telescope has meant a concentration of wealth and rule by an oligarchy. I am very familiar with oligarchy, but I believe you presume you have democracy. (What do I know about democracy? I lived in the 1600s.) My social media telescope reported very little use of the term oligarchy. [1]

Perhaps you have not yet lost democracy. If not, you may still have a slim chance to change the center of gravity from corporate-centric to citizen-centric and turn back the massive unraveling of your society's founding core principles:

Economics based upon brotherhood.

Spiritual/cultural enterprises working out of freedom.

Rights/politics based upon equality.

---

[1] http://en.wikipedia.org/wiki/oligarchy.

MONSTERS THAT KEEP US SAFE KILL US

WHO AM I?

Even when we turn on Turner Classics or the Movie Channel or are streaming the *Game of Thrones* and we are sure there is no one here but us, we still know there are monsters in the world. They are raging against us each and every day. We gave them life and now they rage against us and fill our lives with dread. We made them.

GMOs, TSA, erectile dysfunction, leaking panty liners, heart-healthy cereal, fracking wells, security leaks, IEDs: they come from every corner.

Protection? Even the protection is monstrous! Nationwide drops trees and air conditioners and this causes us to worry about those large pines at the back of my tiny lot. Those pines are on my neighbor's property. Progressive Insurance wants us to take the gizmo to compare. Even the little green lizard has used a mnemonic so we will remember. There is no escape. Perhaps the freezer bags with the extra seal zip-lock top?

WHY ARE THEY HERE?

We are here because we are one world, one MONSTROUS inter-connected world. Coca-Cola can re-use that jingle, but they won't. It's a throw-away. It'll wind up on the beach or in the ocean. Everything winds up in the ocean: miles of plastic bottles, consumer culture, duh-oh! Grow the economy. Grow China's economy, but not Ukraine's or Russia's. Who owns who? Global society requires that I consume what Mexico produces. Legalized, recreational marijuana in Colorado has meant unemployed pot growers in Tijuana. And poppy growers in Afghanistan could care less.

Escape is not a possibility. We can't assign this to James Bond. There is no one evil power. As Walt Kelly reminded us in *Pogo*, "We have met the enemy and he is us."

WHAT DO THEY WANT?
Scotts Turf Builder is demanding I feed my lawn twice a year. "Feed it!" the little Scottish guy demands in a brogue. The Brits are back and want me to buy a "Jag-u-wire." There is no relief. In first-person shooter games they just keep coming. The Toaster Strudel kid is yodeling: "Kandahar."

Has this mayhem reached a now constant level of drone in the background? Can I expect to have to endure this day after day? Are the cable channels the soundtrack my life? American hustle. Uh-huh, I'm afraid so. Just deal with it. Everyone has a strategy for dealing with it. Just grow really, REALLY thick skin, like scales. A dragon skin on the outside and not caring on the inside. Numb. Oh roar a bit in anguish now and then, you're entitled. Maybe blast with flaming e-mails or hyperbole blog posts.

So in the end, we turn ourselves into thick-skinned, roaring, flaming monsters to protect ourselves from the other, roaring, flaming monsters we have created.

Perhaps we should arm ourselves.

DEVOTION BECOMES SACRIFICE: THE SEED OR *THE CALENDAR OF VIRTUES*

The Calendar of Virtues is a year-round listing of virtues in transformation that is linked with a calendar of the natural year. The working hypothesis is that while outer nature is going through its transformations, our inner lives are going through analogous changes. You may post your experiences on the Calendar Of Virtues blog as a part of the action research to see how, or if your inner experiences and virtue transformations link up with nature. Since the research is conducted monthly, this will be slow wisdom that is built up over time. www.calendarofvirtues.blogspot.com

WHO AM I?

I am the seed. I am all about devotion. In me I have bound together all of the genetic matter required to reproduce my species. This has been gathered over successive generations of plants. Some qualities have stayed, others fallen away over time. And I can protect this special cargo for a very long time. Because I am a plant seed, I have enclosed the germplasm in a very hard seed-case.

Human devotion is a virtue and gains strength when one spends time with something or someone important to you, including your future plans and dreams. Like the seed, a practice of devotion is an active gathering together of all the knowledge, insight and experience possible within yourself, and this can take time, lots of it.

WHY AM I HERE?

Sacrifice. The seed is all about devotion and sacrifice. When the time is right, I have got to be able to transform myself, to sacrifice one form (the form I am most comfortable with, have spent so much time perfecting) to become another. I have to sacrifice my beautiful hard shell to become reborn as a plant. I'm gonna need some help. When I'm planted in the dark earth and broken down by water, warmth, and life in the soil, that to which I have been devoted will be released. Without sacrifice the new and improved me cannot be reborn.

Self-sacrifice is terribly uncomfortable. Sometimes, if you are in the midst of personal change, it can actually feel as if something within you is dissolving, something hard or fixed is breaking down.

THE OPPOSITE: NOT CARING

The virtues of devotion and sacrifice depend upon care. There is a risk that they can draw you in to a type of hyper-devotion such as dogmatism or fanaticism. To guard against these excesses, many may develop a negative virtue of distancing themselves by not caring, or cynicism. The soul question is how to stay objective but devoted and engaged, how to come close without merging.

WHAT DO I WANT?

The questions I ask myself are: Has devotion been easy? Hard? Has it gotten stuck? And how is it going with your self-transformation? Is it time to practice the virtue of sacrifice and give up that to which we are devoted so that something new can come into the world, and into yourself?

I AM THE PAUSE BUTTON ON LIFE

WHO AM I?

I am the gap, the pause, the time-out, the recess, the break, the praylaya, the moment between systole and diastole or stimulus and response. The sliver of a second when the pitch leaves the pitcher's hand and the batter commits. I am the "uh-oh" moment AFTER you've committed to a huge force like gravity, or love or a fist-fight, an action you can't undo. I am all these things EXCEPT you are able to consciously step into that gap before the pitch arrives, before you fall down the rock face, plant the kiss or the punch, and are able to stand between cause and effect.

WHY AM I HERE?

This is not about time; it is about timing. It's about being able to imagine forward and backward and see the gaps in time. It takes practice. In German this is called the *rückshau* (rook-shau) and it means "back view." Rudolf Steiner (1861-1925), a social scientist, recommended the practice of reviewing the day in reverse each evening before going to sleep. You literally imagine your day like a motion picture going backwards.

If you can keep yourself from falling asleep, you will see yourself in an objective fashion, like an actor in your life, and know those moments, the gaps, the instances of choice or decision in which you DID NOT pause but plunged ahead. "Oh, yeah. That was when I said that REALLY thoughtless thing to that waitress. Why did I do that?"

Why in the world would anyone want to do this? Because in those tiny, habitual hardly-ever-noticed slivers of time YOU, the authentic you, becomes visible to you, just for an instant. Heartless, cruel, thoughtless, generous, kind, whatever. But you have to disconnect the chain of events in order to see them, and going backwards does this.

WHAT DO I WANT?

Much of life today is on automatic pilot. Trains of cause and effect, pulling cars loaded with habitual thought, leave our stations bound for a one-way journey to a predetermined outcome.

The gap, the pause, is all about freedom. We at least should be free in our heads and responsible for our actions if life otherwise has us boxed in.

I AM GRASS: AN ANALOG FOR YOUR IMMIGRATION AND ENVIRONMENTAL PROBLEMS

"A people without a history is like wind over the buffalo grass."
—Sioux Nation proverb

WHO AM I?

I am grass, 20% of all vegetation on earth, 10,000 domesticated and wild species. Our cereal sisters sustain your easygoing life, perhaps 20% of your economy. Our family is one of the oldest on earth. True grass, the *Poaceae* (also called *Graminae*) the cereals (corn, maize, wheat, etc.), bamboo and varieties you use for lawns. Cousins are the sedges (*Cyperaceae),* rushes and others. You do not know your history with me.

Anglo-European paranoia over grass started with the name "lawn" from the Middle English word *launde,* which originally meant an opening in the woods. Owners of English mansions created artificial stretches of lawn, without trees, to provide an open view of approaching hostile attackers. This was your first, and is still, your prevailing environmental and immigration attitude: someone wants to do you harm so you'd better dominate them first.

The prairie grasses were some of the mightiest grasses on your continent, 10 feet high with spectacular waving seed clusters and graceful leaves that towered over you. In the late 1800s you cut them deep with the John Deere moldboard plow, massacred the prairie grasses, turned over the belly of the earth and called yourselves sod busters.

In the Roaring 20s your Department of Agriculture, pushed as they always are to try to make profits for American industry, attempted genocide on grasses, promoted widespread use of herbicides in chemical farming and promoted the rapid mechanization of farms with small tractors and combine harvesters. You stripped the Midwest and what land was too rough to plow; you overgrazed in a decade of environmental shame.

Some farmers in Europe saw the decline immediately. They asked Rudolf Steiner about non-chemical agriculture, and the agricultural world split. Most went the chemical-industrial path with its mono-culture economic models, hybrid seed and scientific management. Others went the qualitative and environmentally concerned path to Bio-Dynamics, and developed organics as we know it today.

The payback for foolishness was quick. In the U.S. the 30s was a dust bowl with gigantic black blizzards blowing topsoil hundreds of miles. It devastated America's heartland. Farms were lost. Lives ruined. Suicides were common. And why? What was learned as the result of destroying part of nature's fabric, the grasses? By the 1940s former Secretary of Agriculture Henry A. Wallace lamented the tragedy as only a bureaucrat could and waxed eloquent about "the strength and quiet of grass." Your economy was only saved only by a military industrial complex which caused more deaths in WWII.

By the 50s no lessons were learned. All this was forgotten. You never embraced grass but assigned grass to sports fields and tract houses and indiscriminately sprayed the roadsides. Your militaristic spirit led to spraying DDT from airplanes, which resulted in widespread environmental damage and a *Silent Spring*.

And still it continues today through your agro-chemical industrial world economic domination, forcing a so-called green revolution on poorer countries that has caused environmental degradation, farm failure and farmer suicides as massive as those of the 30s in the U.S.

And consumers have been silenced at home and told GMOs are "the same as other plants." Sure. So how is it detectable in breast milk? What will it do to children? And now global warming. Isn't there something about carbon uptake from grasses you haven't heard about? Bamboo is grass. "The wind over the buffalo grass."

WHY AM I HERE?

It was St. John the Baptist who said that he was come to bring a new way of thinking. I too am here to change your thinking about grass and immigrants. You can take a medicine, St. John's Grass (also known as St. John's Wort), to change your thinking, as it is commonly used for depression. I bring you new views of grass from other peoples.

The first view you have is your historical one in which my huge and historical family and species have been killed, dominated and imprisoned, an analog for the U.S. approach to native peoples and immigrants: You also define them by their economic use and marginalize them.

The second view of grass is that of the Aztecs. They honored my family and designated grass a goddess. "The 12th Day of the Aztec tonalpohualli calendar is Malinalli (Grass) and is governed by the god Patecatl, the Lord of the Land of Medicines, a deity of healing and fertility. This day signifies tenacity, rejuvenation, that which cannot be uprooted forever. Malinalli is a day for persevering against all odds and for creating alliances that will survive the test of time. It is a good day for those who are suppressed, a bad day for their suppressors."[2]

The third view is that of the Far East, where bamboo is a food, home building supply, medicine, artistic material and religious artifact. So pervasive is bamboo that the Eastern peoples live in and have settled their lives with grass. You could have done the

---

[2] http://malinche.info/blog/?page_id=34.

same because following WWII, the world's preeminent bamboo agricultural research and development center was in the U.S. That has all disappeared because of competitive pressures for crop subsidies.

So here you have the situation: one people sees grass, the environment and immigrants as something that should be feared and controlled via economics. Another people sees grass, the environment and immigrants as having spiritual/cultural values different from theirs but is wise and sees that those values may be needed in order to change and to survive; values like tenacity and rejuvenation, or grit, for example. A third people integrates itself into the being of grass, the environment and immigrants, and becomes a melting pot. Each of these three were appropriate historically but are now one-sided in their own way. They must be integrated.

WHAT DO I WANT?

I want to show you a final picture of the difference between many peoples' view of technology and the reality of nature in which grass plays a significant role. One of the Hiroshima Maidens said that she was told that grass would never grow at ground zero in that city after the nuclear blast. Day by day she painfully walked with all her injuries to ground zero. She said that when she saw a blade of grass she knew that grass represented a force of healing in the earth that was stronger than the man-made technology of death.

You must know your history. Grass does. Grass has always grown over and covered the horrors of man's battlefields: Little Big Horn, Gettysburg, Hiroshima, and all the rest. And we will grow over your remains if your culture is not sustainable. We know the world's history. And we want to work with you to change your future. Come. Speak to me. Have hope. You know where to find me. After all, don't you say, "The grass is always greener"?

DANDELION WINE: ALCHEMICAL BATTING PRACTICE

WHO AM I?

I am just an old guy with a paper grocery store sack out on his lawn at dawn on May 1, plucking dandelion flowers, dealing with creaking knees and sciatica. I always hope to fill the sack quickly, but the repetitiveness of the task makes it tedious to me and I have to focus on what I'm doing. That is my part of the alchemical nature of the process, having to overcome tedium and remember the lofty spiritual process which I am undertaking. While I am picking I try to think about next winter's solstice, how dark and cold it will be at that time of year and remember all the blinking ice and snow, which melted only a few weeks ago here in New England.

As the kids begin to drift by on their way to the middle school up the street, I realize just how slowly I have been working having to remember all these things as I pick and keep reminding myself I am doing a mighty alchemical transformative task, a spiritual task.

Picking is a spiritual practice, I tell myself. Just like Miguel Cabrera does batting practice in order to win a Triple Crown, I do my spiritual practice in hopes of having a spiritual experience. Can't make dandelion wine without picking.

When the kids ask, "Whatcha doin'?" I respond, "Batting practice." And they look up at the house and note its features to remind themselves later where that "old nut-case" geezer lives so they can avoid this part of the block completely.

WHY AM I HERE?

I gather the petals on May 1 because it is a cross-quarter day between the vernal equinox in March and the summer solstice in June. On or after May 1, alchemists for centuries have said that the dew on the plants after dawn is a holy essence. Knowing this adds meaning to the task. All of this is about adding meaning to life.

At the vernal and autumnal equinoxes the sun and moon stand with their arms out wide and balance the days and nights. Coming out of the kind of winter we had this year, that was a significant marking point for many of us. Winter lost its grip. Now we are facing a long summer which many feel portends drought in some parts of the country the likes of which has not been seen for decades.

The dandelion petals drink in the bright, warm sunshine. This is one of the key alchemical components: sunshine, and all it means literally and spiritually. I want them filled with as much sunlight as possible because I will be making wine out of the petals and want the essence of all that sunlight to be released into the wine. Dandelions are also the first flowers of affection and joy that children give their mothers or others, an essence of childhood innocence.

The dandelion wine will be fermented with a special *Saccharomyces* yeast and, in the six months between the summer solstice and the winter solstice, I will call upon the Queen of the Saccharomyces to transform all this: the dandelion petals and the sunshine they have absorbed, holy essence, the love and joy of the children around the world, the thoughts of the alchemist and added sugar (or honey) while doing her mysterious work.

In my basement work area I add all of these ingredients, stir, pound, squeeze and do all the other techniques; while holding all other thoughts in mind as best I can, I add purified water and call upon the Queen of the Saccharomyces to come and multiply herself thousands of times over to do the task which no person can.

My role is to serve the single cell beings who now do the work. When the primary fermenter is boiling with the cold heat of fermentation, it is frothing and foaming, and the transformation process is well underway. Yeasts are benevolent beings, and if I have made a mistake, they always forgive me. The Queen, like a queen bee, has created a hive of single-cell beings who serve the process and leave nothing untouched.

WHAT DO I WANT?

By the time of the summer solstice the dandelion wine will be out of the primary fermenter and into the glass secondary fermenter. It will be totally opaque yellow to begin with. The opaque plant matter will gradually settle and the wine will clarify. I will siphon it into a clean glass fermenter several more times before bottling it on or about another cross-quarter day in September. Then the bottles will sit in my dark wine cellar at about a 57-degree temperature.

During the winter we give bottles of our wine as gifts. Then, on the winter solstice, when we are already tired of the dark and the cold, we will remember that we have something very special in the basement just for this occasion.

So we will bring up the first bottle and we will uncork it with anticipation. As we sip, the wine releases an inner experience of sunshine and joy within us. We are flooded with memories of the warm days that have disappeared, the warm friends we visited, the bright moments and incidents of the year gone by. Even the dark experiences of the year seem somehow brighter. The mystery is that this inner flame ignites our will and helps us bear the darkness and look forward to the light of the new year about to born.

And each year, I pause to remember that this total process from May Day to the darkness at the winter solstice is in its own way a batting practice for my preparation to enter into the Great Dark of death.

FROM NAÏVE IDEALISM TO ACHIEVED IDEALISM

WHO ARE YOU?

Naïve Idealism is falling in love with an ideal or a person or project that represents that ideal. It takes your breath away, fills you with flaming enthusiasm, ideas, plans, dreams and hopes for the future. At long last you have an IDEAL, a lofty, important purpose. A quest. An impossible dream. You imagine the difference you can make, the unique contributions you can offer, how you can be of service to the project, the team, your lover.

You have been waiting for this. Is this a destiny moment? Your life will be forever changed. You will make a significant gift and, in return, you will be enriched, your life will have meaning and importance. You can almost see the smiles from your loved one or the team. They know what you have done. You can almost hear their appreciative remarks. Those who thought you didn't have the right stuff will, at long last, know your true worth. You made the difference between success and failure, even under tremendous pressure.

WHY ARE YOU HERE?

They will break it to you, and usually not so gently. They will give you a dose of reality. Cold water on your enthusiasm. They've seen your head in the clouds. Heard your vanity. They take it upon themselves to pop your balloon. This is not about you. You didn't have the whole picture. You didn't know the ropes. You were naïve;

that's why it's called Naïve Idealism. It was somebody else's turf all along and you thought otherwise. How presumptuous! Where did you get THAT idea? Somebody else was in control. You were a newbie in a shark tank. Your lover had someone else. Somebody didn't give you what you needed to do it right. You were ill informed. They should have told you before. Now you look like a fool. Feel embarrassed. The ideal is not yours alone. This is not the first time. Why does this always happen to you? Why do you always wind up with the short end of the stick, out of luck, with a bunch of losers who never liked you anyway.

Naïve Idealism (or Love 1.0) is a gift to everyone. You don't have to earn it. It will bring you a picture of what could have been, of your higher and better self, and then that free-and-easy type of idealism shattered that picture. Whoever it was that designed all this was very clever, because you have been left with the three Horsemen of the Personal Apocalypse: Bitterness, Blame and a Broken Heart. But before you ride one of those horses into the world, look around. You'll find that there are lots of footprints out of that lonely place.

WHAT DO YOU WANT?

Rudolf Steiner, that early 20th-century social scientist, introduced the idea of Achieved Idealism in a lecture called *"Awakening to Community."*[3] Steiner says that we are like dreamers who become conscious of our true capacities in this tussle over idealism. It is through others that we awake, and once we are awake, we have to work hard to achieve our ideals through our own efforts. There are so many others who want to take ideals away from us, keep us feeling powerless, keep us unfree.

You want the real deal, you want Achieved Idealism. You have to start with the steel of your personal courage. To make really hard

---

[3] AWAKENING TO COMMUNITY, IX, Dornach, March 3, 1923
http://wn.rsarchive.org/Lectures/AwakeComm/19230303p01.html

steel, called tempered steel, you must heat up and pound the steel. To become wise, you must be seasoned by going through an entire spectrum of unwise actions leading to failure. To love, you must love and be loved. Steiner says it is our community which helps us achieve our ideals and tests us personally, and we need both.

Pick an ideal, the bigger the better: liberty, equality, altruism, religion, democracy, chastity; it's your choice. Then set out to achieve it step by step. Take courage with you and look for others to support you or challenge you, it makes no difference which. Every encounter is an opportunity to learn something about yourself, either positive or negative. Then, based on that feedback, make one small change. This leads to one more quality you need: tenacity. Look at the poem that inspired Nelson Mandela: "*Invictus,*"[4] by William Ernest Henley. "I thank whatever gods may be for my unconquerable soul."

Let us know how you do.

---

[4] INVICTUS - William Ernest Henley
    http://www.poemhunter.com/poem/invictus/

BATTLING DRAGONS

WHO AM I?

Once I lived in a small English village where each year the villagers continue to do battle with a dragon which threatens to consume their teenage children.

By the time the village children have become high school seniors, they know the gossip, the bitter sniping, and the lurid tales of their classmates and the fears and failures of the adults in the small town. They see the results of affairs, drunkenness, drug use and violence.

The dragon which threatens these kids is built up by all of this cumulative old stuff which can kill your enthusiasm for life. Unlike the dragon in fairy tales which is kept outside town in a mountain cave, this dragon is kept locked in each villager's heart – including the teenagers' - and hidden with very polite social mores, mild-manners and stiff-upper-lips. But it is still a dragon and will gnaw at the kids from the inside with fear, doubt or cynicism.

According to the tradition of this place, the dragon must be brought to the out into the open, at least symbolically, and confronted once a year giving the high school seniors the opportunity to confront the beast. This initial facing of the dragon seems more important than the outcome. (I frequently fail in my dragon battling and have developed, over time, a certain tough skin and resiliency as a result.)

The longest day of the year is June 21 – Mid-Summer's Day also called St. John's Day. St. John is the one whose message is transformation: "change your thinking" - change your old reptile-brain, "click-bang" thinking. An auspicious day.

In this community there is a large soccer field not far from the main school building and at the end of the field, near the forest is a large area where the dragon is battled. Starting in the spring whenever someone in the community removes a fallen tree, takes down an old shed, discards old wooden furniture, is ready to get rid of a broken friendship, busted marriage, dumped partnership, drug re-hab, incarceration, specific fears, acts of cowardice and failure – all this old stuff is hauled to the site.

Approximately 2 weeks before the bonfire or roughly the 1st week in June, a group of young men under the direction of several of their elders, will go to the site of the St. John's bonfire and begin assembling the bonfire pyre. On most years there is enough material for a bonfire pyre that is roughly 20 to 30 feet in the air - just about dragon size.

WHY AM I HERE?

This is my first dragon event since I moved here a few months ago from a major U.S. urban city. It is a beautiful night. Many of us ate picnic dinner in the long twilight.

The daylight faded slowly on this longest day and night came upon us. We stood until it was REALLY dark. Without a word, a wall of flame appears at the other end of the soccer pitch. In a few moments you can recognize it as a single-file string of people carrying torches proceeding from either side of the pitch to meet in the center. Apparently there is nothing so ancient as the soul's response to torches – my gut twists.

We hear their voices far away as they sing a St. John's bonfire hymn, hesitantly at first and then a fat girl with bright red hair and a powerful, Janice Joplin voice booms out: "Rise up oh fla-me! By thy light glow-ing!" The line of torches begins to move in our direction toward the pyre. The crowd moves aside. Fear begins to creep up my back. This seems a bit, oh, I don't know, unsettling.

As the song breaks into a multi-part round, the torchbearers begin to weave in patterns: circling, crossing, basket weaving, flames dancing over their heads. Fires balanced at the end of sticks.

And on they come. When the song ends they proceed in silence. As they get closer I can see their faces. Some are grim. Some are fearful. Some must be worried about hairspray. I can pick out faces. The neighbor girl who babysits. The young man from the petrol station. They encircle the pyre.

Abruptly, dramatically, they stop. They stand in silence. Then they turn and face the pyre. They sing one last verse – "Rise up, oh fla-me!" Then in unison they lower their torches to shoulder height and silently begin softly stepping towards the pyre. We watch silently as the torches are inserted into the pile. Then the torch bearers slowly back away.

Then we wait. I see little flickers from within the pile, like a giant egg in which something inside is being roused, waking or being called into life.

The flames begin to leap higher and higher and lick further up the pile of wood, become animate and each flame folding into wings that fly up and up the stack of wood. The being of this fire is born and is taking over what was fixed, consuming it and transforming it. What was hard, solid, recognizable old chairs or doors, heartbreaks and feuds become more fluid as they burn. The flames begin to link with one another and appear to be larger and larger wings than they once were a few moments ago. There comes to be a ring of fire that is running around the outside of this pile of wood and emotions.

And the teens watch as all the old stuck things of their parents flame up like a 30-foot tall dragon with large arching neck and immense mouth – what could have eaten on them up for years on the inside is now out and looks us over.

My God the heat is immense! We back away.

WHAT DO I WANT?
Looking up, I see the dragon wears a crown of flames. And as the flames rise higher and higher, so does the anxiety of the older people who are watching this spectacle. They think that the solid pile of wood and misdeeds has been built up so that it will collapse upon itself and fall into the center. Or at least it is hoped that it will fall into the center rather than fall onto the crowd, causing a tragedy. I imagine a headline: "Man torched by his own flaming arrogance!"

I do not trust fire. Man should not trust fire. Fire is a totally different critter and will look for any opportunity to demonstrate the fact. This dragon certainly seems like it has malevolent potential. But the bonfire DOES collapse back upon itself in a shower of flames and sparks that rise into the air like a million fireflies.

I look upward and watch the sparks fly to the north. And I see through the sparks to the constellations beyond and recall that Draco, the serpent, coils around the North Star, sometimes called the Guide Star. It seems that we must always be contending with dragons in our path.

As the sparks ascend, a thought descends. Everyone except ME knows what comes next. And everyone who knows what will come next DREADS what will come next because I hear the quiet worried comments. What will come next is that the teenagers will confront their own natural fears by leaping over what is now a 3-foot-deep pile of glowing logs and village anger with a hundred eyes winking and tongues of flame flickering.

A clump of four or five young men push through the crowd and people move aside to let them through. The young men stand and consult with one another and point at the pile, apparently planning. Opposite them, across the fire, is a group of classmates, mostly young women, laughing and making "We'll catch you!" gestures.

Then suddenly one young man, the one with the most bravado or arrogance or courage, bursts away from the others and runs full-tilt toward the pile. "Too soon!" a woman says. We villagers are all mentally doing the calculus of fear: his speed, the width of the fire pit, his take-off point and height of his arc, and conclude instantly that he'll never make it.

And he doesn't. But he sees a log in the middle and hits it but, it is not firm, it does not hold, it rolls and we all see the look on his face. Another sphincter tightens.

The boy calculates his options, tries another step on another log, which also gives way; he dives and does a shoulder roll beyond the burn point. The crowd cheers. He bounces up grinning and slapping his pants cuffs to make sure he is not on fire. His friends high-five him.

"Welcome to the world of leaping over old fears and facing dragons," I say to myself. I recall the look on his face. It's the look I have and many of us have monthly when we realize that between medical bills, car payments, mortgage and our daughter's birthday, we're not going to make it over the burning pile in the maw of our financial dragon. So we deal with it.

And on into the night it goes. The teens each face their inner fears and leap over greater or lesser portions of the dragon. The size makes no difference; the fear is just as monstrous for everyone. There will be many tales of bravery and courage (as there should be from anyone who faces a dragon).

And so St. John's night ends with thinking changed, personal fears confronted and the community dragon slain for yet another year.

As for the rest of us, we go away resolved to face our dragons and perhaps make peace with them.

I AM YOUR NESTED SYSTEM
(LEND ME YOUR HIGHER SELF
FOR A MOMENT, WILL YA?)

I am really sorry to have to bring this very complicated schema up at a time like this. I know you're busy, but I can tell that some of you are struggling with weight loss, stopping smoking ("cessation" as it is called now), modifying a habit, parenting, dealing with aging parents, grumpy colleagues, or angry young people. You simply must be aware of how this nested system works.

You might have heard of something that sounds a lot like this on Dr. Oz, but probably not exactly. I didn't make this stuff up by myself, I learned it. I cannot make any magic claims. This is an operating hypothesis, people, not dogma. Ready? Here we go.

WHO AM I?

I am your nested system.[5] We are five sheaths which are nested within your physical body like a Russian babushka doll. The physical body is sheath #1. In this definition, that physical body is the physical material that is left after you die.

If you're not dead yet, then the life or living part which animates your physical body is sheath #2 and is called the life body. In some metaphysical constructs it is called the etheric body. Beyond these two are containers which are less physically connected with the body.

---

[5] Rudolf Steiner, Lecture #2, "Curative Education." *("Pedagogical Law")*

Sheath #3 starts out at birth as our sense body or sentient body. It is comprised of our experiences with the world, physical and emotional, fight or flight, bumps, accidents, joys of success, things we sense and feel but feelings that come AFTER something happens. It's that place where muscle memory lives. It's the stuff-happens body. But when we get old enough to generate our own thoughts, feelings and emotions like love, hate, fear, attraction, these bits that we build up are added to this sentient body, because thoughts and feelings are experiences, too, and this is then called the psychological or emotional body. Also, in other metaphysical texts, called the astral body. So that's sheath #3. It's all about consciousness; we dream in our feelings and are awake in our thinking.

The next sheath, sheath #4, is called the ego. What do you say about the ego? It seems there are two aspects of the ego: a lower self, the more self-centered or ego-istic aspect that wants to have a continually greater share of life's bounty and sees itself as the most important part of creation (as an attorney told my lower self once: "all money flows toward you." Of course my lower self hired this attorney); and a higher self, which we rarely show to others. This higher self is nourished by creativity and can genuinely say "I." The higher self is influenced by our spiritual self.

Sheath #5 is our spiritual self. Our spiritual self lives in the world of ideals, inspiration, angels and also counter (negative) influences.

Okay. This is the nested system which we all have.

WHY AM I HERE?
Weight loss, of course. Isn't that why you're reading this chapter? There is a law which governs all change of habit in this type of nested system. It's called the pedagogical law[5] and it says that in such a nested system of sheaths the next highest sheath can influence the next lowest sheath.

To lose weight, my spiritual self, which lives in the world of the ideal and inspiration, gets inspired that my physical body should lose weight.

My spiritual self goes to the ego to get the team on board. My ego can't simply say to my physical body, "I am inspired! We're gonna lose weight. Now!" or command the body: "Lose weight!" Nope. Won't work.

My ego must work through the next lower sheath, my emotional/astral, and say, "I know you love chocolate, éclairs, peanut brittle, etc. but higher self has been inspired to lose weight, so I'm not getting any more chocolate." Then the emotional body weeps, moans and complains but will eventually work with the life body and say, "I know you have a physical craving for sugar right now, but the team is working on losing weight. Let's do some walking, eh?" And eventually the physical sheath will shed pounds.

In a nested sheath, you can't skip a step. Your ego has to work its way through each sheath. Fairly unorthodox so far, eh? Maybe not today.

WHAT DO I WANT?
I want to let you in on a secret, so if you haven't bailed by how there is a REAL mystery here, something hidden.

The sheaths that are contained in our physical body are discreet to our own body system. The other sheaths: psychological/emotional body; ego, spiritual self; are available to be extended to others.

As an example: An adult can use their ego working through their emotional body to help calm an anxious child because your ego development and strength is greater than theirs. Your emotional body can influence a child's life body. If you can sooth yourself, you can sooth them. Or if you need to energize a youngster for an activity, you have to work from your own enthusiasm.

One note from an old geezer. Parents, PLEASE! It does no good to drag a wailing child through the mall screaming to the poor tiny child, "Mind me!" because at such a young age, the child doesn't have a "mind" or intelligence yet! But let me NOT fall into lower-self blaming. Rather, let my higher self say to your ego, "Hey, you know, you should try skipping. Make a game out of exiting!"

I AM HEROIN ADDICTION

WHO AM I?

I am heroin addiction. I am 16 years old. I was a sophomore when I was in school. If I still was in school, I would be the most popular girl in my school because I'm fun and I really look hot. Everybody wants to be hot! I'm VERY caring; everyone says so. Everyone who meets me likes me. They think they can be with me twice a week and make no commitments! You think you're better than everybody else? That because you're rich you're immune? You can buy your way into this club, but you can't buy your way out. Nobody's THAT special. The ADHD boys come up and say, Let's do "pineapple" (Ritalin and heroin). Okay by me. The momma's boys want "cheese" (their Momma's cough syrup and heroin so they can take it home). Blow your nose and blow your mind. The pot heads want the "atom bomb" (2-fer grass and heroin in one joint), ka-boom followed by mellow. I'm an equal-opportunity high. Everybody says they like the way I make them feel. I make them feel like they're somebody special. My boyfriend has, you know, shared me with lots of his friends. That's okay. We have a very OPEN relationship. I forgive him. Even girls. I don't mind doing it with girls. I can turn anyone on, ANYONE. I can even take an ordinary person and we fool around together a bit and they will like me. A lot of people know me, pretend they don't, but I know them. What starts out as one date, maybe two dates a week, becomes three or four dates a day. We get to be real GOOD friends. It's 'cause I'm so much FUN!

WHY AM I HERE?

Everybody likes to party! 'n I'm a party girl! I think my boyfriend came on to me because I have this steady job. I'm like a home health aide without the doctor's orders. I've never been unemployed. He was older. He had done lots of other drugs, but he said I was the best. We smoked together and it was 15 seconds of pure ecstasy! One, two times and then I cranked up the volume and he was, well, hooked on me. He was after me all the time. I told him that he might as well move in here because if he was gonna want to be with me 20 or 30 times a day, he might as well just hang out here. But I told him, I'm a business woman, a professional, and he had to bring the money. Things aren't going well with him now. He's losing it. He's getting strung out. Begging me. He is just a little TOO obsessed with me, and always wants more and more. That's no fun. I'm a party girl and I'm a little bored with him. And there's this other guy who takes me out to the mall. He buys me cute skirts.

WHAT DO I WANT?

Besides being pretty and a party girl and all about fun, I also have this steady job. I can afford some very nice things. I've got a couple of girlfriends who are pregnant! I could imagine being pregnant. Maybe that's next for me. Lots of girls I know are getting pregnant. They can call me Auntie. I'm thinking about having a baby. I love their LOVE-a-baby showers. I think a lot about babies, you know. Baby shoes?! Don't you just love BABY SHOES? I'm just addicted to all those baby clothes. I'm real busy doing my thing so I'd have to get someone else to take care of the kid. I hope they don't cry. What a bummer; a crying baby makes you want to smack them. Maybe you'll come help take care of my baby, share the love. There's plenty of love to share.

IS THE DEEP SPRING OF YOUR CREATIVITY IN DEEP WATER?

WHO AM I?

I am the deep spring from which your creativity once flowed. Like all springs, I come from a source. In healthy ecosystems there is a continual renewal process so that deep springs do not go dry. But maybe you've forgotten this process, or think it is not important or that you are not responsible for the maintenance of your creativity. Or perhaps you believe you can neglect it because you've ALWAYS had the touch, the spark, the juice. Do you think I appear by magic? That I'm a gift that will keep on giving? Hello!

You use your deep spring like a lawn sprinkler, in a centrifugal fashion. You, my friend, take my creative flow and use it in your life. Do this, do that, do the other, always creating, always tapping into the flow of spirit. Output, output, output! Do you even know how much creative juice you had in the first place? Never thought about it.

Friend, that creative flow has got to come from somewhere! Your spring has a recharge process. Oh, gosh, you thought you got an unending supply of creativity and magic stars without having to do anything? What is going on in the spiritual world's pre-birth prep process? I know life is a do-it-yourself process, but a creativity expiration/sell-by date printed on your feet would help. Where's that suggestion box?

Okay: recharge processes 101.

WHY AM I HERE?

The deeper springs and aquifers in the physical world have a recharge process that is just the opposite of the lawn sprinkler. The sprinkler is a centrifugal or output model. The recharge system is centripetal and requires an even larger catchment area or watershed of spirit to flow in and refill the aquifer or spring.

Physical systems are replenished or recharged by rainfall or snowmelt. Some springs, quite near the mountain snow-pack, may be replenished after winter, so their recharge rate would be a few months. The giant aquifer in the Midwest, the Ogalalla, is said to take 100 years to replace every 1 inch of water that is drawn out. Sustained drought and depletion of water resources have made the regions around the Sahara desert even more barren and have begun to affect even the deep wells in the region.

Look around. Is the environment around you nourishing to your soul and spirit or causing you to burn more creativity just maintaining stasis? Rather than a carbon deficit, have you got a creative deficit? Architecture and color are vital, as in vitality. What about play? Is there any physical play possible? Ping pong, stationary bike, darts? Can you relax into at least one area of your office or home?

How is it with you? Are you feeling a bit thin? Do you have what it takes to reach down to bring up the juice for an especially challenging situation or opportunity?

WHAT DO I WANT?

What is creativity made of? What recharges you? Time. Medical research has shown that it takes at least seven continuous days for the average American worker to be recharged from the stresses of their jobs. How many continuous days off do you take each year?

Time is the secret ingredient driving your physical capacity for health. This translates into cardiac variability, the capacity to handle stress. Repetitive, dulling patterns of behavior kill your capacity to adapt. And what is adaptation? Creativity, sometimes called play.

What is the recharge rate for your soul? Are you near sources of renewal? Do you actively manage your soul recharge? When is the next play date on your calendar?

Where can you find a well of time? How can you recharge the deep spring of your life? Time, in as many variable forms as possible. Sunrise and sunset. Seasons. Gardens are filled with time. Children: putting kids to bed and reading one chapter. Music. Surprise parties! Laughter! Dancing. Reading. Play. Sleeping late. Rising early. Any and all time-based activities break the habitual routines and bring creativity. Live, laugh, love.

Otherwise, your deep spring is in deep water.

NICCOLO MACHIAVELLI AND RESURRECTION FORCES

WHO AM I?

I am Niccolo Machiavelli. My treatise, which separated politics from morality, was called *The Prince* and was published in 1513. The brand has done very well! Only a modern mind would apply a then radical concept, amorality, in so many practical policy ways at all levels of society worldwide!

This year is the 30th anniversary of Ronald Reagan's and Oliver North's (two great American patriots) Iran/Contra dealings. Reagan said publicly he'd never deal with terrorists. North diverted funds to terrorists and summed up the situation with language that sounds as relevant today as it did 30 years ago: "There is great deceit, deception practiced in the conduct of covert operations. They are at essence a lie. We make every effort to deceive the enemy as to our intent, our conduct, and to deny the association of the United States to those activities. . . and that is not wrong."

Only you have now applied this principle exponentially and everywhere! Well done! You still have the powerful 1% which govern the 99%, or, as I called them in my day, "the mob."

The way I put it in *The Prince*: "All men will only see what you seem to be; only a few will know who you are, and those few will not dare to oppose the many who have the majesty of the state on their side to defend them....For the mob is always impressed by appearances and by results; and the world is composed of the mob."[6]

WHY AM I HERE?

I stopped by to remind you where your modern thinking comes from. You don't call them princes, you call them governors, but they will soon be saying: "What are you thinking? We can't decriminalize anything. We're certainly not going to let an entire generation of black men out of prison because of a little thing like overly harsh drug penalties, are we?"

Remember, it was me who said: "I say that every Prince ought to wish to be considered kind rather than cruel. Nevertheless, a Prince must be indifferent to the charge of cruelty if he is to keep his subjects loyal and united."

Forces of amorality go hand in hand with brutality. And you have media today, something I DIDN'T have! As I always said, "…a Prince should make himself feared in such a way that…he escapes hatred; for being feared but not hated go readily together.…And if he finds it necessary to take someone's life, he should do so when there is suitable justification and manifest cause.…pretexts for taking someone's life arise more rarely and last a shorter time."

Your media and networking and the brilliant law that says corporations are people make so much more possible today, for who can really attack a corporation for corrupting the land, seeds or food? Not even your government. Justice bows to economics.

WHAT DO I WANT?

Ah, what a long strange brand development journey it's been; the memories tumble together! The big dogs of racial, religious, political and economic levers move cultures around the world: Black Panthers; Red Brigades; Soviet-style ethnic cleansing in Yugoslavia

---

[6] *The Prince*, D. Donner tr., Bantam Books, 1981.

and Rwanda; eco-terrorism; Jewish settler massacres; gang wars in Mexico; Waco/Branch Davidians; trade union massacres; race riots; MOVE bombings; Chinese Communists; South Africa spying; Rodney King; 9/11; priest sex scandals; pipelines; GMOs; the Arab Spring; financial plundering; no jobs, no future, with the complicity of princes of all sorts.

The modern age has learned the lessons of amorality well.

But there is a final lesson which princes do not want to hear and so will overlook. A lesson they find incomprehensible. There is a force more powerful than their amoral politics, economics or false religions because it comes from the heart of man.

I wrote, "...when the people begin to look upon a thing with horror, they will persevere in that attitude for many centuries, but princes will not do so." And over the years I watched this perseverance and suffering at the hands of Princes and something happened. I beheld the power of transformed horror.

A prince should never forget that artists take in the forces of amorality, the horror, death and brutality, and transform them into art. And when they do, their art has resurrection power.

You princes and people, look around, can you see this resurrection art appearing and transforming the bitter into the sweet?

GO DOWN, ARCHETYPAL MOSES

WHO AM I?

Recently I flew from San Francisco to Washington, D.C., leaving SFO at 5 p.m. and arriving IAD at 1 a.m. I had to catch another flight at 8 a.m. I was too cheap to spend the money for a few hours in a hotel room. "Not enough time," I thought. So I spent the night in the airport sleeping on the vinyl benches.

The whole surreal experience reminded me of Dante's description of one of the rings in *Purgatorio*. With the dim fluorescent lighting, I couldn't even cast a shadow like a Shade. It put me in touch with homelessness. I realized that a great deal of our lives are lived in these in-between places where we have to spend time, the waiting rooms of life.

That's why I admire my wife. She's a knitter and a resourceful, practical person. She keeps herself occupied. Apparently knitters do not suffer the agony of waiting. She just kept click-clicking away. Knitters were not mentioned by Dante. (But knitters should not get a big head; they weren't mentioned in *Paradisio*, either.) Eventually the clicking of her needles only added to my misery.

If I feel I do not have enough time to accomplish any one of my very self-important tasks, I'll sit in dull resentment. Rather than play computer solitaire, I'll apparently take sub-loathing in *Purgatorio*. Not in the dark. Not in the light. Not quite living. Not quite dead. To paraphrase Kris Kristofferson in his song "The Pilgrim," Not quite truth, not quite fiction, "a walking contradiction...taking every wrong direction on his lonely way back home."

WHY AM I HERE?

Self loathing is boring. What does one do in such a situation? And there are lots of us: the unemployed or underemployed, temp workers, callbacks, the wrongfully incarcerated, those awaiting medical tests or treatments, those who must wait.

Well, I always think about archetypes. Don't you? Archetypes are the real deal. They are the truth, even if they are fictional. The original.

The first. The mold out of which each and every copy is formed. Each archetype has the full power, the undiluted truth of the form. The full-tilt boogie.

Archetypes live in an infinite reservoir of meaning and power out of which the streams of imagination flow. There is also the water table of archetypes into which one can tap when stuck in IAD for six hours.

When you deploy an archetype, pick one that is really dramatic and interesting, because you have hours to fill. Rather than stay with Dante's *Inferno,* which I explored in my play *Dante in Jiffy Lube,* I called in Moses. Whether you portray Moses in a 6th-grade play or sit in the presence of one of Leonardo's sculptures, your ticket gets punched forever. The experience is your ticket to revisit that archetype at any time.

WHAT DO I WANT?

Moses helped me move from my specific fate to the general and heightened my interest in the godawful Pharoh airline scheduling plague. You look at your experience of Moses as an archetypal lens and, through interaction with archetypal forces and principles, things change.

Languishing in the gray airport gloom like the children of Israel who had missed their last flight to the Promised Land? Enter Moses. Need a little leading of your ancient Hebrew soul out of Dulles or Egypt? You bet. "Burning bush" to fire things up? Why not? Let's get some enthusiasm going for Starbucks opening in four hours! Some laws? "Thou shalt not schedule flights in such fashion!" Born a slave and want to become a rich guy? Still a slave and feeling oppressed? Have become a rich guy who is out of touch with your people? Call down some plagues on the neighbors? Had a plague called down on you? We can all relate to SOME aspect of the archetype in some way.

Even when our whole lives seem to be lived in between, in some waiting room for the next phase, or in recovery, or we have been sold into bondage in some fashion, archetypes can guide us and give us new ways of interacting with our fate. They are universals, which means they are recognized and understood by others. They give us answers or provoke questions. This is why they are so powerful. They are common currency for ideas, ideals and feelings, forces and principles.

"Go Down, Moses!" is a gospel song that I first heard when I was just a kid. I sang it when I was working that midnight shift for UPS and I was bone weary. You hum it (this is the "interaction" part), trying to soothe yourself on the benches at Dulles, or at least I did. Sing slave songs when we feel oppressed.

Having said all that, while the archetype of Moses was comforting me on my bench, I must admit that the one courtesy blanket I found stashed in a closet was worth its weight in archetypes. Lucifer kept the a.c. blowing all night in that particular corner of Hell.

THE STRUGGLE FOR THE NEW FAITHFULNESS

WHO AM I?

I am the things that control you: I am the saros (the sun and moon barycenter) which, through the courtesy of the *Suprachiasnatiuc Nucleus* (SCN) of your cells, links your body to the circadian rhythms of day/night. I am the geography of where you live or work. I am the cultural system of your people, tribe, gang, clan, corporation, neighborhood, school or work place. I am the local, regional and national economy. I am the political system, national, state and local. I am individuals who have power over you: your parents, family, friends, enemies (whether they be naturally connected or blended by relationship or by karmic carpool.) These are some of the exogenous (outer) systems that control you.

I am also your endogenous drivers: your age and phase of development, your place in birth order, your body limitations (weaknesses and strengths), or the addictive substances that control you. I am your DNA, your biology and your medical history. I am your inner personality fragments which drive you psychologically; your compulsions, fears, doubts, anxieties, repulsions, attractions, habits, temperaments, memories, syndromes, dreams, chemical reactions to pharma and psychological manifestations.

And then there is your spiritual dimension, your openness to spiritual influences; your religious shaping, your destiny, which somehow filters your perceptions and is a type of oscillator that excites you or turns you off.

Our age is quite pleased that it has defined a human being in such intimate detail.

WHY AM I HERE?

All these things control us and define us to one another. They offer easy labels by which we can categorize one another with our quick scientific minds. Then we think we know one another. And because we have this modern orientation that likes simple categorization, and because this is a time-pressured era, we sum each other up in simple phrases: little boy, old man, working mom, heart breaker, wise guy, or any of a dozen more. They are the stereotype, the shorthand picture.

When you meet me, when I meet you, we must work very hard to find one another amid all the baggage we carry, the complexity of who we are. Within all of these dynamics is the genuine you and the genuine me.

One of the tricks for actually meeting one another is to reverse our wills. When we sit together, I say to myself, this is not about me, it is about you. I am here to serve you. What do you need? What's up with those rings? I can grow curious about you in the space I can create within myself. And if I sit quietly and ask simple, simple questions, out of that very dynamic person you are, from that complex baggage and history, a very unique person may emerge, even just for a moment.

WHAT DO I WANT?

I want us to try to tame one another and offer a space for that very unique other to feel safe enough to emerge out from within the complexities of themselves. To TAME one another, like the fox in Antoine de Saint-Exupery's *The Little Prince*:

"To me, you are still nothing more than a little boy who is just like a hundred thousand other little boys. And I have no need of you. And you, on your part, have no need of me. To you I am nothing more than

a fox like a hundred thousand other foxes. But if you tame me, then we shall need each other. To me, you will be unique in all the world. To you, I shall be unique in all the world....”

Meeting or taming is the first step toward a new FAITHFULNESS that Rudolf Steiner describes:

> *Make for yourself a new and strongly courageous view of Faithfulness.*
> *What is usually called Faithfulness passes so quickly.*
> *Let this be your Faithfulness.*

> *You will experience moments, fleeting moments, with the other person, when he will appear to you as if filled, irradiated, with the true essence of his Spirit. And then there may be—indeed there will be—moments, long periods of time, when he becomes dried up and darkened. But you will learn to say to yourself at such times, “The Spirit makes me strong. I remember the true being of this person. I saw it once. No illusion, no deception shall rob me of it.”*

> *Battle always for the image that you saw. The struggle is Faithfulness and in this struggle one person shall be near another, as if endowed with the Guardian forces of the Angels.*[7]

---

[7] *TruthWroughtWords*, Rudolf Steiner Press

THE REBELLION AGAINST
THE GOD OF MYSELF

WHO AM I?

For a long time I thought that when I prayed or received an insight or inspiration, I was speaking with God. It turns out that, apparently, I was speaking to my angel, my spiritual self, and not God.

I discovered this recently when pain took over a portion of my body and a large portion of my attention and it became clear that the ME that was always in control and responsible for EVERYTHING was no longer in control. Pain, like an arrogant angel, refused to obey ME, the God of Myself.

This rebellion shattered my trust. Our body is built up out of trust of seamless experiences of life. We trust that from one day to the next things will be pretty much connected as they had been. Even after injuries our bodies adapt. This builds up TRUST IN LIFE, a fundamental, very deep existential trust in the FABRIC of life and it is related to your experience of the world. This trust in life can be shattered with a significant illness or injury. This rebellion against the God of Myself was significant.

WHY AM I HERE?

From a certain perspective, my physical body was the ground of my world, the lower order of life, my tradition, and the religious establishment of myself. It seems the same for others. On this we build up our psyche, our identities, our personalities, our biographies. So the rebellion of the obstreperous angel of the body triggered a response.

It is not unusual for maturing men and women to weep for their lost youth. Many of us have clung to hopeful fantasies of future accomplishments. (My bucket list includes climbing Longs Peak just once more and this *sciatica* put that at risk!) These are woven from our bodies. I harbored and whispered these hopes to myselves (important personality fragments: Jean the teen, Jean the 20-something, etc.) when we were alone. These myselves emerge as our *doppelganger*, our soul double, and stand beside our angel.

My higher self, my double and the obstreperous angel of my body walk into a bar. This is not a joke; this separation of physical and spiritual can be powerful and can deepen the feelings of loss of trust in life or self-confidence. It can happen at any age. This is precisely the moment when many start drinking or doing drugs. Some because they feel failure and give up (flight); others because the ego wants to prove that it is more powerful than addictive substances (fight).

But addicts will tell you that they escape from addiction only through a moment of clarity (the gap we explore elsewhere) and self-reflection with the help of others. This is true for us all.

The automatic trust in the fabric of life, in the protective power of guardian beings, is gone. Like the sentient beings we are, you beat us once and we will be apprehensive. Beat us twice and we know who you really are. There are no illusions about the future.

I asked the simple question: Why have I arrived at this place? Why am I here? Perhaps it is this moment of clarity.

WHAT DO I WANT?

Objectivity. All of this has earned me a certain freedom from myself. I am liberated, a little bit, from me. My body is a little bit more broken and willing to let go. I have begun to step away from the God of Myself. My doppelgangers and I are doing a bit of sorting out. Gaining this objectivity will be essential for my being strong enough to consciously participate in the next steps. Our role is to NOT be a passive victim but to be response-able, alert and responsive like a wrestler in the grip of, and gripping, a powerful opponent so tightly that you can feel the muscles beneath the skin. We are one in a struggle. Wrestling with this angel will prove to have been an important factor in determining the course of my revelation. Living spirit is never bound to tradition; it blows through the channels of experience in our lives as it will.

The following verse has been helpful to me.

"For the Michael Age" also called *"Meditation for Courage,"* by Rudolf Steiner

> *We must eradicate from the soul all fear and terror*
> *of what comes towards us from the future.*
> *We must look forward*
> *With absolute equanimity to whatever comes*
> *And we must think only that*
> *Whatever comes is given to us*
> *By a World Direction full of wisdom.*
> *It is part of what we must learn during this age,*
> *Namely to act out of pure trust*
> *In the ever present help of the Spiritual World.*
> *Truly nothing else will do*
> *If our Courage is not to fail us.*
> *Therefore let us discipline our will,*
> *And let us seek the awakening from within ourselves,*
> *Every morning and every evening*[8]1

---

[8] This struggle is universal and is detailed by Rudolf Steiner in his book *Esoteric Science,* Section V, Cognition of Higher Worlds, part 2. http://wn.rsarchive.org/Books/GA013/English/AP1972/GA013_c05-02.html.

APPARENT NECESSITY

WHO AM I?

I have an awkward question about wars, school shooters and office supplies.

The spectrum of evil slides from the really big stuff: conscious environmental degradation ("vital for the survival of our way of life"); pernicious capitalism ("major profit-taking today"); theocratic sacrifice ("protect tradition"); school shootings ("I showed 'em"); and so forth, all the way down through Congressional action/inaction ("The President was OUTRAGEOUS!"); Presidential actions ("I had to act!"); through state government ("pre-emptive laws"); to schoolyard bullying ("He looked at me funny"); and family squabbles, to crimes, slurs, and all sorts of petty wounds and attacks, not to mention impulse sales and an entire retail industry of consumer goods. All are primarily driven by one thing: APPARENT NECESSITY.

WHY AM I HERE?

I am once again at Staples. In my case, I have some sort of inexplicable urge for office supplies. Not necessarily to buy because I've run out of something, but just to wander and see new pens and stuff.

Apparent Necessity works like this: Someone gets the idea into their head to do this, that, or the other, regardless of the consequences of their actions, because they feel it is NECESSARY for them to take this action. It's not necessarily a compulsion to act immediately, like payback, but it becomes an apparent necessity.

Or it can be pleasure, like an affluent person who shoplifts or engages in risky behavior that they apparently find necessary.

Where do these thoughts or feelings come from?

Is there a default setting in our souls based on some sort of deficit built up over time, which can drive us, consciously or unconsciously, to take action to resolve this need?

And who or what is it that triggers the action by whispering our unique pass-code? "Office supplies, Jean...office supplies!"

WHAT DO I WANT?

The term "unrighteous" is a really interesting one that you don't hear much these days. Wonder why? Unrighteous means: not right, not fair, hollow, empty, unsupported by law or custom, unreasonable, or unjust. (Merriam-Webster also included "wicked," but it seemed a stretch to get to "wicked" from office supplies.)

There are a lot of actions by a great many people reported by the media today that are said to be not right, unjust, hollow, empty. (Okay, following my quick mental review, the reports included some wicked things, too, so I'll put "wicked" back in.)

Let's see if I can review why I'm once again in Staples: Each human has some unique form of default setting, a personal inner lack or deficit which we personally strive to correct or repair; and this is also the means by which systems such as advertising, religion, finance, business, politics, culture, sex, and so forth, manipulate us by offering something to relieve our deficit. ("That embarrassing itch!")

And if the actions we take as a result of seeking to fulfill our personal needs are self-centered, shallow, wasteful, empty, hollow, foolish and so forth, then are not our actions unrighteous?

Awkward.

And aren't those systems that prey on our weaknesses and manipulate us (fine tuned by psychology, media, marketing and sales) so that their apparent necessities are secure even more unrighteous?

More awkward.

And they prey on other enterprises in the same way, exploiting their fears and shortcomings in order to consume them or manipulate them for gain. Is this not also true?

Really awkward.

But apparently, here in this country, it is necessary for us to continue to live this way, because this is the way we live, right? (Hmmm. A tautology. Awkward.) And living this way is apparently necessary to someone.

WHY IS BIG BIRD BIG AND YELLOW?

WHO AM I?

Good morning. I am here to present our original research for Children's Television to you, the newly formed Broadcasting Advertising Council. This research was carried out in the late 1940s just before televisions were mass marketed. This was baseline research on consumer use of the technology. These are the fundamental science-based building blocks for the huge, successful growth in children's television programming and brand development.

The very first phase of our fundamental research sought to understand the relationship between children and the new technology of television.

May I have the first slide, please?

Here you see a home-style living room with a mixed group of children ages 3, 4, 5 and 6 and a large Philco television. Look closely. What do you see? You see the children PLAYING, playing with blocks, model cars, the cat, tossing the bean bag, ANYTHING but watching the television. At the very beginning of our research, this was the fundamental relationship between children and the technology of television: children simply weren't interested! The world was too attractive and they were too curious. These were children whose normal response to life is to play! (Cute, aren't they?)

Next slide, please.

WHY AM I HERE?

Here you see another typical living-room set with a mixed group of children ages 3, 4, 5 and 6 staring raptly at a large Philco television. Why? Why aren't they playing? We have captured their attention.

How did we do this? Through behavioral research we discovered various visual and audio techniques are more powerful than reality and could be used to make the children focus their attention on the screen: brightly colored characters, particularly those that are distorted in some way, either bizarrely large for the small screen, with feathers or fur, brightly colored; or with fantastically large heads, or big mouths, and so forth. And sounds are, of course, strong: distorted voices, sound effects or associated noises are most effective.

We tested each of these techniques across the U.S. and included "DISTRACTION TESTING," to make sure that we could hold the attention of a child for up to 30 minutes at a time. Distraction testing is, of course, where the children are sitting in front of the television and, at the precise moment a character or action we wish to test appears, we create a disturbance in the room, say a spilled bag of candy. If any child goes for the candy, we revise the character and re-test until we have total child attention on the screen

Next slide, please.

WHAT DO I WANT?
This is a cut-away of the typical television set showing the cathode-ray tube.

The final part of our research will explore the effect of the scanning cathode-ray tube on the brain. While the behavioral devices defined by our research have proven to be highly effective techniques for drawing children's wandering eyes away from reality back to the screen, we believe it is the television tube's scanning technology that holds the children, indeed all viewers, mesmerized.

As you know, there is actually no single picture on a television screen, just phosphorous dots arranged in 250-line bands which are illuminated a few at a time by the scanning cathode-ray gun. For the same reason children love to play, because they are naturally curious about the world, the child has an in-built compulsion to make sense out of the flickering phantoms of light, to solve this technology's sensory puzzle and complete the picture. Neuroscientists hypothesize that to do this the brain is hyper-energized and works so hard that television both captures attention and sends the viewer into a vegetative cognitive state.

The electronic baby sitter and teacher and marketer!

Children are learning! Your advertising has used the techniques I have reviewed today and I'm pleased to report that 5- to 7-year-olds have successfully recalled products and performed well on brand identification tests after only a few exposures! Who says kids aren't smart? I'd say that this will be the key to America's future! A generation of trained consumers!

So, gentlemen...and lady, you stand at the threshold of a new consumer America! And we will be very happy to include your products in our testing array.

Thank you for your time.

THE HELMSMAN ARISES

WHO AM I?

I am the Helmsman, the steady hand on the rudder of your life, your guide, your pilot over the most dangerous environments, the forces of the unknown, of potentials dwelling in the sea of your life. I am that self-image you have created who is so confident, self-assured, in control. When asked, "Can you…?" the Helmsman answers, "Of course," even though you know you're double-booked. But, somehow, your Helmsman guides you through the crashes, the bumps, the hurt feelings or late nights. Your Helmsman does not want anyone to think ill of you.

We Americans love the Helmsman archetype; it is one of the most dominant and revered in our culture. It surfaces in all popular action-adventure shows as a detective, surgeon, soldier, crime scene investigator, the risk-taking reality show cast member, Hell's Kitchen chef, and so on. The steady hand on the tiller, the master of the craft. "We got this."

We Americans love those who are in control of their technology, any and all technology. We believe our technology is our destiny. In former years the Helmsman was the cowboy, and the technology he controlled was horses and guns. Even Shane said, "A gun is just a tool."[9]

Technology brings the Helmsman into advertising. The Marlboro cowboy was the quintessential Helmsman. The cool-eyed lady behind the wheel in many car commercials is a Helmsman; pushing

---

[9] SHANE, Jack Schaefer, 1949 en.wikiquote/wiki/Shane

buttons, shifting, speaking commands, handling groceries and children and arriving early. Even diseases and addictions are easily handled. Erectile dysfunction? No problem: call the pharmaceutical Helmsmen. Depression? No problem. Advertising shows us how to be the master of our fate, the captains of our souls; the sales event ends soon.

WHAT DO I WANT?

Many of us don't want to be a Helmsman; we want to follow one. We want to ride on that craft and have someone else's steady hand on the tiller. Is your Helmsman a technician? Are you betting your mortal soul on their technology? Will you, like Dante, choose to follow a poet? Or, like Lewis and Clark, do you follow a Lemhi Shoshone woman like Sacagawea? Do you follow a star? A theology or a priest, a mother, a goddess? Does an affirmation guide you? ("Every day in every way I'm getting better and better!")

What will you pay your Helmsman? There is always a cost, whichever path you take. Even if you pay with increased stress levels, hypertension and weight gain, you pay. In the Greek myths, Charon, who took the souls of the dead from life into the underworld across the river Styx, had to be paid, otherwise a soul wandered the shore for a 100 years. In Goethe's fairytale "The Green Snake and the Beautiful Lily," the ferryman wanted no gold but only fruits of the earth like artichokes and onions. Even Willie Loman's wife commanded that the stars pay attention. What will you owe your Helmsman if you give him immense power over you?

WHY AM I HERE?

The Helmsman arises because we as a culture are afraid. Most Helmsmen stories are simple stories that deal with fears. Media want the simple stories. Young people want results. They grow impatient waiting for answers. Simple stories get produced on TV and film; complex stories don't.

Young people are satisfied with the Helmsman. My Helmsman has gotten me into and out of many scrapes when I was young, too. But now, I feel as if my Helmsman is morphing into the Ancient Mariner, and passengers like you and me roll the dice with death.

I'm a Baby Boomer, and the simplistic Helmsman stories fit less and less each year. Many of the classic images of my generation were Helmsmen, but they are old now and tatty around the edges. Perhaps I've seen too many of them.

My generation's lives were once blown offshore to outer adventures. Now the winds of age for many of us have come about and now blow inward. Sometimes there is a double direction, outward and inward. Now many of us are on an inward journey toward death. This is very new to us, and we are apprehensive how this will pan out. Life has gotten complex. The inner journey is fearful.

In actuality we are up against anonymous, faceless and extremely complex realities that will kill us. We long to imagine bad guys getting what they deserve, as in most classic Helmsman stories.

We want Clint Eastwood as Dirty Harry atop our killer, waving his pistol and saying, "C'mon Cancer, make my day!"

Or Gregory Peck as Captain Ahab, with his harpoon lashed to our White Whale, saying, "Alzheimer's! You die!"

Or James Bond confronting our arch enemy, hypertension, who, in the style of Auric Goldfinger, says, "No, Mr. Bond, I expect you to die!" just before Bond shoots out the plane's window, which depressurizes the cabin and sucks the villainous clogged arteries into the sky.

Simple Helmsmen may not handle the dynamics.

Perhaps it is not too late for us to take on an ancient, richer archetype like Odysseus; who followed, or invented, multiple Helmsmen, some true, some false (lies), some himself, some others, at different times in his journey. Sounds like just another Boomer self-delusion, eh?

I AM YOUR KNOT, THE STRUCTURE OF YOUR REALITY

WHO AM I?

Two lives bound together in a knot.

The first life comes into being from one direction, family, location, with one intention, and then goes over the other person and then under them. The second life comes from perhaps a totally opposite or at least a quite different direction, culture, family, life intention and goes under the first person and then over them.

Each pulls in an opposite direction until they are tightly joined in different intentions, past and future, love or hate; physically joined, or emotionally knotted, or spiritually bound. This knot is called a square knot because there is reciprocity to it. It's a square-ness, as in equality; pull on a square knot and the tension is distributed equally.

In a knot, if one individual pulls from one direction the other individual will feel the pull, the constriction, the tension.

Two lives bound together in a knot. Is it created out of love? Out of karma (whatever that is)? Out of being two people whom life puts together and bonds with personal chemistry?

WHY AM I HERE?

Explore the knot.

Love is a meeting of two people with attraction to one another. Tension, perhaps sexual at first, holds the love knot together.

If love is not passionate, the knot will be too loose and the union will fail. But if sex is the only strand in the cord, it will fray and break over time.

Karma also is a force of attraction coming from the past, even from action of others, like family. Tension holds the karmic knot together because there is a desire to discover why the relationship exists.

Karmic knots will be tested as well. There must be juice. Some reason for being united, positive or negative, will be learned.

Why *this* knot? Knots have special purposes. A square knot is different from a bowline, which is used for heavy lifting. That is different from a sheepshank. What kind of knot are you in? Knots have intention: mutuality, control, constraint, lifting, carrying, or easily offering freedom to untie. Why *your* knot?

If a knot is too tight, it will bind and not be flexible enough to accommodate the pull of a person's life.

Knots are not permanent; they are the power relationship between those who are joined. Knots can be tied and untied. They are complex and complicated dances in space and time.

Do they feel like bondage? Unions are about relationships that will not last forever. Human freedom must not be bound. How long does love last? Must karmic debts be repaid? Explore the knot.

WHAT DO I WANT?

Two groups of people bound together in a knot.

"It really boils down to this: that all life is interrelated. We are caught in an inescapable web of mutuality, tied into a single garment of destiny. Whatever affects one directly, affects all indirectly. We are made to live together because of the interrelated structure of reality."—Rev. Martin Luther King, Jr. (1929-1968), Christmas Sermon, 1967

How does this "inescapable web" between people work for you, personally? Do you feel yourself caught in such a "garment of destiny"? What are its characteristics, physical, emotional, or spiritual? Can you draw the knot, this soul macrame? Objectify it?

Where is this knot or garment too tight? Too loose? Too loving? Too hating?

What is the history of this garment? Who tied and who may untie these knots?

The "single garment of destiny," this "structure of reality," is comprised of multiple threads that are affected by the knot. Yet each human thread has free will. Who will stand and tighten their cord and pull with others in a different direction? Who will loosen and love?

ABOUT THIS WORK

"From Naïve Idealism to Achieved Idealism"
"Fabulous...inspiring and true. Thank you!"—W.E., Author of six novels

"I Am Galileo and Facebook is My Telescope"
Dear Jean, pardon my density, but I'm not sure what this all is. Exciting idea, but being as literal-minded as they come, I think I need more. Is this a free-form experiment to see what comes up in the net when you haul it to the surface?—T.R., Vermont woodworker

"I Am the Tongue of the Liar"
"Thank you for that trenchant *"Tongue of the Liar"* blog. Very timely!!"—E.S., Waldorf educator, author

"The Helmsman Arises"
"Well...Kill the Helmsman...Or maybe at least retire the Helmsman to the vault of past dream movie. Nice bit of writing...."—J.S., Detroit-based film producer

I like it, Jean. I missed the working mother helmsman (or woman?), though. The one who says you can do a top notch career-building job while raising kids and maintaining the household at home. Talk about stress! Ulysses? One of my favorite poems: *"We are not now that strength which in old days/Moved earth and heaven, that which we are, we are;/One equal temper of heroic hearts,/Made weak by time and fate, but strong in will/To strive, to seek, to find, and not to yield."*

—D.A., Vermont English teacher

"William Shakespeare and You Dream Each Other"
"This gnaws at me."—Anonymous

ABOUT REFERENCES TO RUDOLF STEINER IN THIS BOOK — I worked from 1997-2007 as Administrative Director of the Anthroposophical Society in America, supporting local study groups of Rudolf Steiner's spiritual research methodologies. Steiner, 1861-1925 was a PhD in Natural Science and a spiritual researcher. The world headquarters is in Dornach, Switzerland.

Printed in the United States
By Bookmasters